"Countless individuals have opened the door;
it's the courageous who walk through it."

~ Tim McLeod, Alumni Relations Manager, Sierra Tucson

NOTHING
CHANGED
but me

Real Recovery Stories
48 Hours After
Leaving Treatment

Published by Sierra Tucson Publishing

ISBN: 978-0-9994430-0-2

First Edition

Publication date: November 15, 2017

Printed in the United States of America

SierraTucson.com/NothingChangedButMe

Acknowledgments

We wish to express our deepest gratitude to those who supported the creation of this book from Sierra Tucson Publishing.

We dedicate this book to those who accepted the call to work with struggling individuals and families. You are the heroes. As agents of change, you show up day in and day out to provide hope and healing. If not for you, this book would not be possible.

We would like to express our deepest appreciation to Bill Anderson, Sue Menzie and Jaime Vinck, for their unending encouragement and support of this project. Lisa Jane Vargas, for her leadership and incredible optimism throughout this project. Alison Broderick, for her copy editing talents. Courtney Martinez, for her help getting the word out to source stories. Gina Kilker, for her part in conceptualizing what this book could be, for interviewing contributors and editing their stories, and for coordinating the project. Chellie Buzzeo, for the endless hours she spent creating the interior and the cover of this book, in addition to all her publishing guidance. Cindy Hutchinson, our incredibly gifted copy editor. Our PR Team at The Lavidge Company, for their efforts in promoting the book. The entire Sierra Tucson Alumni Advisory Council, for sitting in a room and opening their hearts and baring their souls that one fateful day in May, 2015, which led to the creation of this book, that we know will support many who have been to treatment, and those still to come. William T. O'Donnell, Jr., for his vision in starting Sierra Tucson in 1983, and for his belief that we all have the capability to find the miracles within ourselves. And finally, Tim McLeod, the driving force behind this project, for always believing that these stories matter, and that *every* person's recovery story matters.

As always, we express our greatest respect and admiration for each person who has walked through the doors of Sierra Tucson to seek change and departed to reclaim their life.

We are proud to be part of Connecting a World of Miracles®.
Alumni Relations / Sierra Tucson

As a professional, I have had the gift and opportunity to work with those who are just considering recovery, all the way to those who have chosen to live life in long-term recovery. As a person in long-term recovery, I understand how essential hope is to getting from one to the other. The stories shared in this amazing book have the power to connect with people wherever they are on their journey of recovery by showing there is hope and that recovery is possible. Recovery = Change.

Patty Reyna, CARC; CPS, CRPA, RCP

Man, I wish I had had this book in 2004 when I was getting ready to discharge from Sierra Tucson! I was nervous and felt so alone after spending an intense and intimate time with my cohort in the desert, sheltered and cushioned by Sierra Tucson magic. The idea of going through the same treatment center might give one the impression that all the people who have completed the Sierra Tucson program have had the same experience, but we haven't. We lived on the healing grounds and felt the structure that was created to cultivate healing, but each alumnus and current resident goes through at different times, with different staff and different ownership, and we each come from such different backgrounds, our wounds do not look the same. So when we pass the "You Are a Miracle" sign as we head out the driveway of Sierra Tucson, we each have a completely unique set of emotions, expectations, fears, thoughts, urges...and we each find ourselves faced with the very thing that Sierra Tucson warned us about and tried to instill in us: now it's up to you and God. And so our recovery journey is set in motion. What a wonderful gift to have this book, to hear the voices of the healed and healing spiritual ancestors who came before us on this journey – sharing their experience of those first 48 hours. If you're reading this book, I wish you well, good luck and Godspeed.

~ Tiffany Spilove, LMFT
Eating Disorder & EMDR Trauma Therapist

Some things you cannot argue with:
There is safety in numbers.
The truth always shows up.
Recovery is a lifestyle, not a graduation.
Relapse is a choice, not an accident.
It's OK to say "it's not OK."

And grateful people never fail in the recovery process.
We can whine or shine, it's up to us.

This book describes very clearly the beginnings of
health, wealth, gratitude and grace that will continue only if
we CHOOSE them over easy, sleazy, queasy or please me! Find
the time to read what is shared here, then pass on what you
discover. We can never keep it to ourselves when others need it
so badly. Yes, that's right...

Someone needs to hear it from YOU!

If you have some, give some. If you need some, take
some. Every story in this book has a nugget or seed of truth
that works for recovery on a daily basis and was developed and
strengthened in the first hours of leaving residential treatment.
What you give energy to...will continue. Period.

Hugs and hope,

~ *Mark Lundholm*
Comedian

I am so inspired by these stories; they remind me of
the days of my own early recovery. There is power in how
we remember our struggles and triumphs. Thanks to Tim
McLeod and Sierra Tucson, we can share this unique collection
representing those truths laced in courage and hope.

~ *Carver Brown*
Alumni Coordinator
Pine Grove Behavioral Health

Nothing Changed...But Me is the real deal! After over 30 years in the recovery field, I understand the importance of the first 48 hours post-treatment. This book portrays "reintegration" as it is—scary, exciting and often humorous. I really enjoyed the way the authors addressed the most important part of recovery—the first word of the First Step —"We." Thank you for the honesty and courage to let others know they are not alone!

~ *Paul J. Gallant, MC, LPC, CIP*
Primary Recovery Services

Stories are the heartbeat of healing and recovery. We have all lived through difficult versions of the human experience only to discover, through others who have come before us, that we are not alone. *Nothing Changed...But Me* is an inspiring look into the beauty and struggle of the change process. It serves as a healthy reminder that those of us with the courage to reconcile our past is not what is wrong with us; it's what is right with us. Sierra Tucson remains on the cutting edge of alumni and aftercare services, and this book is another innovative opportunity to improve outcomes and change lives.

~ *Miles Adcox*
Chief Executive Officer
Onsite

5:49 AM

"The ever-amazing
Santa Catalina
Mountains. I came to
believe while walking
on the trail that
they could handle
my problems....

9:02 AM

I imagined
the pioneers
crossing them
and the problems
they must have
left behind. The
challenges they
must have faced....

2:06 PM

I grew to love those
mountains, ever stoic,
filled with beauty,
always changing....

4:09 PM

A cloud covers them
for a minute and the
top is covered with snow,
and moments later,...

4:13 PM

the sun is laying
its beautiful rays
across the valleys in
ever-changing patterns
of light and shades
of green....

8:12 PM

They became my Higher
Power and I would miss
them so much. They
showed me a path to
spiritual peace. Would
that exist at home?"

~Janet S.

NOTHING
CHANGED
but me

Real
Recovery
Stories
48 Hours
After
Leaving
Treatment

I left so happy to have
30 days alcohol-free.
I had never been
able to achieve
30 hours without wine,
let alone 30 days.

In anticipation of going to Sierra Tucson,
my goal was to achieve 30 days of no wine.
Even though I didn't know what to expect,
my experience at Sierra Tucson turned out
to be so much more than I anticipated.

I surrendered, I guess.

Surrendered to something
I didn't know or understand
on a drunken plane ride to a place
I had never been, to spend 30 days
with people I did not know.

The most impactful thing I heard when
I arrived was from the medical director.

He said,
**"A paradox:
Sometimes the
thing you think is the
worst thing in your life
becomes the best."**

Preface

In May 2015, a group of men and women, each of whom had experienced recovery at Sierra Tucson, gathered together. A real estate developer, a tech guru, a full-time mom and now recovery specialist, a retired hospitality industry executive, a human resources benefits specialist, an heir to a family business enterprise—none of whom would have had much in common under normal circumstances, yet their paths were intersecting—united with a common goal. As with most people in recovery, they understood one another better than perhaps most of their own friends or family could. After all, they spoke the same language. They experienced the same trials. They had lived with the same hurdles of hopelessness.

Consequently, they were asked to contribute and to be part of an important gathering. The challenge before them was this: How could individuals leaving treatment be even more supported? What more could be done to show them the love and care they felt while in treatment in Sierra Tucson's residential care? It was the brainchild of Alumni Relations Manager Tim McLeod. Always working to boost alumni involvement and improve support, Tim knew this group of six wouldn't just brainstorm ideas; he knew they would openly share from their hearts to reveal their own experiences, and then draw from those to grow Sierra Tucson's efforts to reach more alumni.

True to Tim's vision, the meeting was emotional. These were people who sincerely wanted to give back, and by giving their time and ideas, they truly were. Dubbed the First Annual Alumni Advisory Council Meeting, an idea emerged. It sprung from an overwhelming consensus, a feeling that tied them—and perhaps all alumni—together, that Sierra Tucson saved their lives. As they collectively looked back at their individual experiences at Sierra Tucson, they discovered they each had anticipated dread and fear at the prospect of leaving when their treatment concluded. Each admitted that upon discharge, leaving the safety of the Sierra Tucson "bubble" was akin to trekking into a vast, unknown, and frightening territory. Had they known then that others who had gone before them had also felt the same, they agreed that that fact alone would have provided great comfort. That's when the idea of sharing the real stories of alumni and their first 48 hours outside of the safe cocoon of residential treatment, was born.

> *"Leaving the safety of the Sierra Tucson 'bubble' was akin to trekking into a vast, unknown, and frightening territory."*

This book is designed to help those who are in treatment today and are looking ahead to that day of discharge. It is for family members to understand what to anticipate as their loved one returns home from treatment. It is for those who have left treatment and need to be reminded of just how far they have come, or, perhaps, how far they still need to go. It is also for those of us who need to be reminded that the spirit of recovery and healing indeed begins to take shape and bloom in the most unlikely places—where the dark root of fear and self-doubt thrive, and where that side of ourselves that we don't want anyone else to see, lives, breathes, and, too often, commands our attention. And lastly, it is for the very human part of all of us who think we cannot do what seems impossible to accomplish.

Although the book title describes that the stories focus on the first 48 hours after leaving treatment, many of these stories incorporate much more than those first two days. As people shared their stories, they revealed the experiences that had shaped their lives and had landed them in recovery, and what it means to them now, all with the hope of helping those who come after them. As you read these very personal accounts, we know you will agree that no matter where we are in our personal journey, there is a lot to be learned.

Thanks to all of you who shared your stories of how your change began. We honor your experience and are grateful to you for adding to the legacy of recovery.

6:42 PM

Sierra Tucson...
The Vision

We all have important work to do in this life. For me, getting sober, taking care of my family, and helping others have been where all my efforts over the years have remained. Like anyone who will be reading this book, I lived a life full of suffering and pain fueled by my addiction, until I found the gift of recovery. Recovery can be a difficult journey, but with commitment and effort, life becomes full of connection, meaning, and purpose!

Again, perhaps like many of you, after years of struggle I was fortunate enough to seek help and entered treatment. Prior to treatment and recovery, I had worked as a successful executive in my father's company, but I knew that things would need to be radically different than they had been in order for me to truly be successful in seeking change. I learned a lot from my education and business career, and, just as importantly, I now had strength, hopes, and experiences that I could call on to create a new life.

In 1983, I went to Tucson, Arizona, and became a partner in the treatment center called Sierra Tucson. My vision was born out of my own treatment experience, and the many wonderful patients and staff who were there for me and gave me inspiration. But I knew that in order for Sierra Tucson to become a special place, I needed to move beyond the old 28-day model. Drinking and drugging have always been symptoms of the problem or the disease of addiction, and most patients have more difficulties and issues than just "not drinking and using." That's why our approach from the very beginning was to address the "whole person" in a highly individualized manner. It was not the one-size-fits-all method. We believed and understood that addiction is a family disease, and the entire family became an integral part of the treatment experience and healing process. Along with many of the great traditional treatment approaches, we provided specialized groups and education, with a strong emphasis on experiential modalities such as equine-assisted therapy, mind-body exercise, healthy diet and nutrition, and a host of other services, which at the time were considered cutting-edge.

My hope is that all of you, whether you have been part of the Sierra Tucson family or not, continue to be inspired on your journey and, as they say, continue to Pass It On.

~ William T. O'Donnell, Jr.
Founder of Sierra Tucson

The Commitment Continues

Change. For some, that word stirs up excitement, opportunity, and growth. For others, it provokes fear, anxiety, and pain. Yet change is inevitable. People experience change, from year to year, day to day, and moment to moment. I believe the beauty of Sierra Tucson, as founder Bill O'Donnell had envisioned, is that residents experience change in a very healing way.

Written on the sign as one enters Sierra Tucson are the words "Expect a Miracle." This powerful message informs those seeking help that a change is coming. Not a small, minor shift in perspective, but a radical change—a rift in how one views life. A miracle is about to happen—to them!

Our commitment to Bill O'Donnell's vision has not wavered. In fact, I believe that it has been invigorated. We are as focused on creating a therapeutic environment as ever before. We believe that change is the cornerstone of the healing process.

Since 1983, Sierra Tucson has helped more than 33,000 individuals discover a new way of living. We continue to be thought leaders and pioneers in the field of mental and behavioral health. Part of our commitment to helping residents find recovery is to provide support after residential treatment, which includes a full year of continuing care and a lifetime of alumni services. Sierra Tucson is committed to connecting a world of miracles by continually exploring new ways for providing additional support.

Alumni Relations Manager Tim McLeod is a gift. His passion for Sierra Tucson is unparalleled and contagious. When Tim proposed a book that articulates the struggles within the first two days of leaving treatment at Sierra Tucson, his excitement was palpable. He was so dedicated to providing hope for those individuals who are newly out of treatment. He wanted to highlight the "change" that happens in everyone. How incredible! He wanted to share messages from caring alumni who had been through this process, giving back to those who have not yet recognized the miracle.

Nothing Changed...But Me is an inspiring book filled with hope and real stories. It is a book about healing and compassion. It is a true account of those moments that shake or rattle the change that has already occurred. It is a testament to the courage and resolve in which people face their recovery. Nothing is more important than finding your miracle, no matter where you choose to seek help.

We Support You.
Bill Anderson, MSW, LCSW
Chief Executive Officer, Sierra Tucson

The Gift

When I came to Sierra Tucson, it was nothing that I expected, but everything I needed. Like others who've had the courage to seek treatment, I came for relief and received a transformation—a transformation that began with my willingness to surrender and be honest. During my stay, I heard the treatment team say repeatedly, "You can't walk a new journey with an old toolkit." Meaning, if I was to expect my life to be any different, then I needed to apply the skills I was currently learning.

Looking back, I would have loved to receive a copy of this book when I was a resident at Sierra Tucson. What a gift it would have been to gain knowledge from those who walked before me. The connectedness I would have felt, knowing others shared my same fears of returning to the real world, would have been a comfort. The greatest gift, if I would apply what I learned, is that I, too, could handle life on life's terms.

I am so grateful to everyone who contributed in the creation of this book.

To those experiencing treatment for the first time or those returning to do more of the good work: remember, you are never alone. You are loved and I support you!

~ Tim McLeod
Alumni Relations Manager, Sierra Tucson

Jeff B.

Upon arrival at Sierra Tucson, I stared at my wristband and immediately focused on the date of my discharge, which happened to be the day before my wedding anniversary. I was focused on being home for dinner that night with my wife. Almost instantly, my thoughts turned to life after treatment....

But it wasn't until 28 days later that I was told I would for certain be home in time to celebrate my seventh wedding anniversary. That precious day was the turning point—the moment that I would set upon a new course in life.

Part of my release process was a final psychiatric evaluation, and as we were ready to wrap up, my psychologist got very serious and asked, "So, what are you going to do when you get home?"

Without a thought I said, "Go out for dinner to celebrate our anniversary!" I was 30 days clean, away from everything, and ready to take on the world. She shook her head and asked me again. "Give my kids a big hug?" I said, beginning to question my answer.

"You are going to find a recovery meeting before you go anywhere!" she said emphatically. Ah, yes! Recovery was about to begin, and now it was on me.

No more schedules, no more supervision; it was time to get rigorously honest with myself and be accountable to my program of recovery without the Sierra Tucson "bubble." I packed up my recovery toolbox and started to learn how it worked in the real world. I checked out before dinner, anxious to say my goodbyes. The golf cart was packed with my possessions. I boarded the same van that had brought me to this magical place. On the way out, we drove past the sign that read, "You Are a Miracle."

My flight home to Chicago was very early the next morning, so I was dropped off at a hotel near the airport to spend the night. Liquor stores, strip clubs, and temptation were right outside my door. This is where I would be left to start recovery. Obsession instantly sprang back into action as I stood at the door of my hotel room, free to choose my next move. I pulled out the first tool Sierra Tucson had given me: play the tape. It reminded me that old thinking would earn me another seat on the van back to Sierra Tucson. So instead, I locked the door, ordered a pizza, poured a Coca-Cola over some ice, enjoyed a bag of Peanut M&M's and turned on the television.

I checked in to Sierra Tucson because, after smoking marijuana daily from the age of 17 to 37, I was faced with termination from my job with the family business, where getting fired was a pretty tough thing to do. I drank when it was not socially acceptable to smoke, perhaps inspired to do so from an uncle who always thought that wine would be a good alternative to being a pothead. Ironically, he died of alcoholism. But I thought differently of that practice when my first roommate at Sierra Tucson suggested that I could not drink anymore either. That bit of advice changed my life. With a desire to stop drinking, I chose Alcoholics Anonymous as my 12-Step program. It was suggested that I give it a chance, so I did. After arriving home and hugging my kids and my wife, it was time to find my first meeting.

I picked a meeting at a local AA clubhouse and left early to find it, not sure of the location. I arrived very early, and as the room began to fill, so did my head with old thinking. "This guy looks crazy. I'm not crazy." "Maybe this is the wrong meeting." "What if there aren't more people?" I dug into my toolbox again and remembered: my best thinking got me here. The meeting began and they asked, "Is this anyone's very first meeting?"

I raised my hand and answered, "My name is Jeff. I am an alcoholic." Miracle!

I was welcomed and treated to a First-Step meeting. I made the time to be there; it was the first step on my road to recovery. Everyone shared with me how he or she got to

Alcoholics Anonymous. It was not about alcohol; it was about life. Each person gave me a glimpse of what life is like now, mostly happy, joyous and free. When it was my turn, I shared that I had just gotten out of treatment and it was my first meeting in the real world. When I was finished, they thanked me for coming and said that I really helped them to remember how hard it was to make that first meeting.

After the meeting, they gave me phone numbers, which I ended up calling whenever I had questions about meetings. Going to a meeting was the first of many things that was suggested to me after leaving Sierra Tucson, and when I did it on my own, it felt great. I knew I could no longer procrastinate in my life. I wanted to find a sponsor in my first seven days at home, and on the seventh day, I did. He suggested 90 meetings in 90 days, so I did that, too. It taught me how to find a meeting and that there was always time for one in your day. He suggested I call him every day, so I did, and each day it was a reminder that I have to take action in recovery in order to keep growing. Following suggestions gave me a daily routine, and I soon realized that I was still sober (and, occasionally, happy!). Sobriety and recovery started to become the "substance" that brought me joy or that helped me to find joy when I lost it.

There are many definitions of the word miracle, but the one I like best is "any expression of love." The magic began when I realized I was a miracle. Continually forgiving myself, and following the simple instructions provided, was essential for me in early recovery. The instructions seemed complicated; yet I found that I had to get out of my own way and ask for help. Staying outside of my comfort zone is where growth happened in treatment and thereafter. Recovery has been painful at times, but I found the hurt only temporary. When I allow pain to become a guide, it leads me to acceptance and letting go. I never have to fear the next decision to be made. I simply choose out of love, and the miracles just keep on coming.

McKinley L.

I have battled depression since I was 8 years old and have been on different medicines and therapies throughout the years. On top of it all I've battled alcoholism; it took me a long time to see it. But finally, there were a number of incidents and a pattern of drinking and blacking out that finally made me admit it....

My time at Sierra Tucson turned out to be a life-changing and truly amazing experience. It saved my life. My mom and dad came during Family Week and so much came to the surface. At the root of my issues was my brother. He has obsessive-compulsive disorder and had been abusive toward me. My mom hid it and my dad never saw it. It was all this abuse that affected me, and at Family Week it came out. Their lack of dealing with and acknowledging it was really at the core of my issues.

After 30 days, when it was time to go, I dreaded leaving. I wanted to stay and extend it to 45 days, but I couldn't since insurance didn't cover it. If I could have stayed, I would have. I was safe and happy. I was healthy and exercising. Plus, I fell in love with the desert. I remember the last few hours of saying goodbye to everyone and giving notes to different people. I thought back on that first morning when I walked outside and there was a giant rainbow right outside the door. I saw it as a sign. I went on a walk around the track. It felt so amazing out there. But here I was now, I had said my goodbyes and left. To my surprise, I didn't cry. I was excited and ready. I felt OK. I got my phone back. Since I hadn't seen it for a month there were a bunch of messages from so many people. They were so supportive. I texted my close friends and family. I wasn't shy to tell them, "Hey, I just got out of treatment. I love you."

I had a driver who drove me to the airport. I checked in for my flight and I remember walking around the airport feeling so alive and seeing things I hadn't noticed before. I felt curious about everything that was around me. I sat at the gate and thought about my homecoming and my dog that I would be seeing soon. I always tell people that he saved my life. During the worst of times he would lie on my bed and be there as my support. His name is Buddha; he is a big boy. I wouldn't have gotten through without him. He is my world. I have driven across the country and even to Canada with him. Wanting to be a photographer, I have started documenting our journey together: "My Life with Buddha."

I am always social on planes. On the plane ride home, I sat next to a young woman who was visiting her fiancé in the Army. I told her I just got out of a 30-day treatment program and she was so supportive and nice to me. When I arrived in Atlanta, I was in the bathroom at the airport and this woman walked up to me as I am washing my hands and said, "Good job!" She had overheard me talking on the plane, and she shared that her son had been battling similar issues. We hugged when we parted. I was vulnerable and honest and received well. The fact that I was helping someone else just by sharing my experiences was really a special moment.

Then I walked out of the airport and was greeted by Buddha and a team of people—my mom and dad, my grandfather and my aunt, and our good family friends. There was a lot of love and support waiting for me; thinking back, I know I couldn't have done it without them. We went out to dinner that night. It was a dog-friendly restaurant and we had a great dinner together on the restaurant porch.

Afterward, on the drive home, I felt clear. I had drank a Coca-Cola at dinner and reflected back on how excited I was at the freedom I was feeling, and thinking how all the stresses of the world can affect my clarity and positivity. I went into those first 48 hours after treatment positive and strong. My goal was to find a therapist as soon as I could. The next day I went to a recovery meeting and got a massage. Things were getting off to a good start.

Eventually, I moved back to Colorado, and during that time I have had ups and downs. I go to Alcoholics Anonymous meetings and practice yoga every day; I even started teaching yoga. Teaching is healing and has helped make recovery positive.

For me, recovery has been about being open and honest and fighting for it. I fought for it by seeking therapy, going to AA, and talking to friends and family. So many people have helped me. My support system was definitely the key to my success. I learned so much about myself when I got to the root of my depression and anxiety and began to understand those triggers.

Looking back, the therapists who have helped me were just amazing. I encourage those who are getting out of treatment to go to a therapist immediately after and continue with it. Stay accountable to someone. This year I went to the Sierra Tucson Alumni Retreat. It was another way to stay accountable and a good restart. Plus, it was a great chance to reconnect. It was amazing and good.

I left Sierra Tucson with a box of tools. I naturally turn to my tools when needed. I go through cycles, but looking at me now compared with where I was before, I can see that I have experienced a ton of growth and change. I still have struggles, but I am sober. I have a lot of work to do, but I have my tools. There are so many times that I don't even realize I am using them. They have become part of my life, and a crucial part of my growth and change.

Andrew S.

When I got to Sierra Tucson, I was at the lowest point in my life. I was going to bed every night praying not to wake up, and then waking up every day angry that I had to do it all over again. I did not know how to end my life; nor did I know how to continue....

Lying on the cold floor of the bathroom in Desert Flower, Sierra Tucson's stabilization unit, dope-sick and depressed, I had an epiphany. Clearly, I did not know how to live life, and maybe someone else did. I decided I was going to be open to the suggestions of the Sierra Tucson staff, and maybe things would get better.

Prior to this, I was not what one would call an open-minded person. I thought that I knew everything, and if only people would do what I wanted them to do, and if only things were the way I wanted them to be, then I could be happy. Consequently, I was a very unhappy person. I did not respect most other people and I was filled with shame for who I was and the bad things I had done.

So I started doing the work that was suggested; I went to all of my scheduled activities, and I started to learn about me and my disease. I worked hard on myself for 30 days. About one week before I was scheduled to leave Sierra Tucson, I told one of the therapists that I was afraid I was going to relapse after I got out. He told me that it was a reasonable fear, and he gave me some very wise advice. He told me that Sierra Tucson was like boot camp. I was learning about the tools that were available to me in my recovery, but I did not have the experience that I was going to need to use those tools. He told me that when I left Sierra Tucson, I was being dropped onto the front lines, and he asked me who I wanted to have around me to help me survive. Did I want to hang out with people like me with little or no experience, or did I want people with a lot of experience and wisdom? I knew I wanted to be with those folks with some time in recovery. My therapist told me that surrounding myself with these people and listening to them with an open mind was the key to laying a strong foundation in recovery.

One of the most important lessons I learned at Sierra Tucson is that I am teachable. I received clarity on the floor of that bathroom in Desert Flower, and I was willing to listen to people who had some time in the program. What a gift and a miracle!

I left Sierra Tucson on a Tuesday morning, and everything seemed strange to me. I went to a grocery store and I felt like I had landed on a different planet. Everything was foreign and chaotic. That evening, I attended a Sierra Tucson Alumni Support Group. I was still carrying a lot of fear, and when I met the people at that meeting who spoke Sierra Tucson's language and supported me, I now understood what my therapist was talking about. I got phone numbers and set up one-on-one meetings with some of the men. They helped me then, and they continue to help me today.

Prior to leaving Sierra Tucson, I had worked out a continuing care plan with my primary therapist. This plan included 90 recovery meetings in 90 days, attending an intensive outpatient program, finding a sponsor and working the 12 Steps with him. So that is what I did. I was blessed to find an amazing recovery community that was willing to help and support me. In the rooms of my 12-Step fellowships (Pills Anonymous and Narcotics Anonymous), I found people just like me.

My first negative thought when I started going to 12-Step meetings was that I was different from the other people at the meeting. I had felt a kinship with the fellow residents at Sierra Tucson that I did not feel with the addicts in the rooms. But after listening to folks from wildly different backgrounds share their stories, I started to realize that they were just like me. When I opened my mind to listen to their stories, I was able to find common ground with every one of them, the same way I had with the residents at Sierra Tucson. I was talking to another Sierra Tucson alumnus soon after leaving treatment, and I told him that I liked going to meetings, but there were people in the rooms that I did not like. He told me that was perfectly OK. I did not have to like anyone in the rooms, but I did need to love them. I did not understand what he meant at the time, but I do now. I was judging these individuals and closing myself off to their stories, and that allowed me to feel different from them. These are my fellow human beings, children of a Higher Power, just like me. If I could not love them, then how could I love myself? I believe that self-loathing and self-judgment are at the core of my disease. Before I got into recovery, I could not stand to be around me, and when I found a remedy for that (i.e., pills), I had even more reason to despise myself and wallow in shame.

When I went to Sierra Tucson, I left behind broken relationships, a destroyed business and livelihood, potential criminal charges and civil damages, and massive debt. When I got out, all of that was still there, patiently waiting for me. None of it got better for a good, long time. However, I got better, and I got better at dealing with it. Most importantly, I got better at dealing with my biggest problem: me. I learned how to cope with me on a daily basis; how to be honest and do the next right thing.

Another miracle is that I wake up every day grateful to be alive, and I go to bed each night grateful for another day clean. By working a program that was suggested to me by Sierra Tucson, I get to live a life filled with love, hope, happiness and freedom. I still have feelings of sadness, guilt and shame, and I still make mistakes. But today I know how to feel the feelings and make amends for my missteps. I would not be alive today if I had not gone to Sierra Tucson when I did. And I believe that every person who comes through those front doors by that beautiful fountain is a blessed miracle, just like me.

Linda S.

(f a m i l y   m e m b e r)

My husband and I left Sierra Tucson just before lunchtime. We went to a favorite place in Tucson for lunch and it felt like a date. I felt happy to be with him and eager to hear all about his experiences at Sierra Tucson. Amazingly, he was willing to talk to me....

He talked about things he learned at Sierra Tucson, and his feelings. His FEELINGS! This was a very new experience for me. I didn't understand all of it, but I was willing to learn. And I was willing to try to rebuild our marriage and our family.

During the ride home, I began to feel anxious. I had set some boundaries during Family Week at Sierra Tucson regarding his return home, and I felt that he had not come clean about everything. It turned out that he had not, and it would take months for that to happen. Now, I know that was an unrealistic expectation, and it had caused me a lot of pain.

That evening, my husband and I attended the Sierra Tucson Alumni Support Group in our area. I thought this group was really just for him and that he had to attend. At first, I went along to make sure he attended the group. I shared in the meeting about my feelings and I was amazed at the loving feedback I received from this group of strangers. I left that night full of hope and gratitude because my husband went home with phone numbers and a future date to meet the group members for coffee.

To support my husband's recovery, I chose to attend Al-Anon meetings as regularly as I could. I had only been to a few Al-Anon meetings and I knew about the concept of a toolbox—resources that aid in recovery—but I didn't know how to use any of them. I said the Serenity Prayer over and over and that bought me a few minutes of peace. Attending an Al-Anon meeting could get me an hour of peace and hope, yet I hadn't found many friends in the meetings and I struggled. I felt fearful, angry, lonely, and sad. I was rarely happy, but I was willing and grateful. And, most importantly, I kept showing up.

In my Al-Anon meetings, I learned that my husband's recovery and whether or not he attended recovery meetings were none of my business. I felt hopeful whenever I was in a meeting but still struggled when my husband and I tried to work on things together. I realized he was getting better and I was not. While he was able to stay calm and have the difficult and painful discussions, I found that I could not. I had a lot of anger and fear, and I needed to work on me. That realization did not happen in the first 48 hours. It took months of progress, not perfection. I kept going to meetings and getting to know the people in the fellowship of Al-Anon. I finally found the courage to get a sponsor and work the Steps, and I volunteered to be of service.

It is a miracle that today I am happy and enjoy serenity more than I ever did before I found recovery. Hard and uncomfortable stuff still comes up, and I turn to the tools of the program to get back to serenity. Sometimes I misplace my tools, but I only need to go to a Sierra Tucson Alumni Support Group or an Al-Anon meeting or call my sponsor to find them again. I am so grateful to the Sierra Tucson community for the experience, strength, and hope that they have shared with me over the past six years.

Lori H.

When I arrived at Sierra Tucson, I felt broken and powerless. An 11-year relationship with an abusive narcissist, who, as it turned out, was also a sex addict, had finally brought me to my knees. The emotional pain had become unbearable, debilitating....

A lifetime of trying to cope and carry the burden of relationship trauma, psychological trauma, medical trauma, car accident trauma, death and loss, was no longer possible. I needed more than my own self-will to survive.

I voluntarily entered the Trauma Recovery Program. I decided I was ready to do whatever it took; ready to let go and fall into whatever dark, scary places I needed to go to heal my pain. I was ready to experience the promise posted prominently at the entrance to Sierra Tucson: "Expect a Miracle."

I remember wondering more than once while at Sierra Tucson, would it be enough? Would it be enough to turn my life around? Would it be enough to save me? I had to find a way to accept that it would be. I had to find a way to trust that the people and programs at Sierra Tucson would be enough to move me forward on my healing path. I heard from others who had gone before me that Sierra Tucson would "plant the seed." It would be a powerful beginning to the rest of my life. And it was.

For the first time in my life, while at Sierra Tucson, I had come to know what it was like to feel safe, to have personal boundaries, to feel at ease in my body. Every evening I'd go out to the field and look at the Santa Catalina Mountains. I'd watch the sunset, the pink glow highlighting every angle of those mountains. I finally felt connected to something bigger than me, the mountains reflecting this back to me. I felt held and supported. At last I could breathe! I came to know the feelings of miracle and abundance. I forged a deeper relationship with, and awareness of, my body. My breath, I learned, was the doorway into my soul, my spirit and my emotions. In the desert of Tucson, I found myself.

Before I was released, my therapist worked extensively with me to craft an extensive self-care program, which was one of the most comprehensive I have created to date. I was told that it would be best not to go home to the environment, relationship, and person that caused the devastation that finally brought me to Sierra Tucson in the first place. It would be like going home to a war zone and trying to continue the healing process. The staff recommended an extended-care facility. Unfortunately, I was unable to afford this, so I had to go home.

The day I was released from Sierra Tucson, I felt vulnerable, open, and hopeful. I also felt dread, anxiety, and fear. I feared that I would fall into old patterns when I returned home, that I would succumb to my partner's pressure and manipulations and ignore my own needs and wants to appease him, to stay "safe." I was afraid I would continue my old patterns to avoid feeling devastation and abandonment.

When I returned home, I felt sadness and frustration for the first few days. Leaving behind such a peaceful, worry-free, structured environment and coming home to traffic, people, noise, and stuff I had to do, was a struggle. I longed for a different reality. I longed for Sierra Tucson. Just as predicted, coming home also presented a challenge in dealing with my partner. Even though he was doing recovery work for his sex addiction, he was still a narcissist and a bully. My trauma triggers and codependent solutions were right beneath the surface, waiting to be used in that old familiar pattern of mine. And then I noticed, in spite of what I was feeling inside, I didn't act on it. I surprised myself by articulating what I needed calmly and maturely. I regularly referred to my comprehensive self-care list and practiced doing everything on it that I needed to do to take care of myself. Because my trauma triggers could cause me to dissociate and made thinking very difficult, that list became my lifeline.

I quickly found a new trauma therapist, found a local Co-Dependents Anonymous program, started going to regular meetings, and found a new women's group more in alignment with where I was in my healing process. I started regular exercise, meditated, practiced my breathing, began my list of how to become less financially dependent on my partner, talked to my friends, and reached out for a lot of support. I asked for help when I needed it, something that had previously been very difficult. All of this was from the seed that had been planted while I was at Sierra Tucson. I finally knew that no matter what, I was going to be all right; no matter how long it took, I would be OK.

In those first 48 hours, people said they noticed something different about me. I appeared calmer, more grounded. I noticed I felt different, too. Even though everything and everyone were familiar, I was experiencing it differently, with fresh eyes. I wondered what was different. Then I realized, I had hope.

Today, I still have hope. My partner and I are no longer together. I remain committed to my healing and recovery process; I have many tools and a lot of support. My trauma triggers and codependency no longer control me. I am not broken. I never was. I was injured. I am finally connected to a Power greater than myself and am happy to say, I look forward to the rest of my life. Thank you, Sierra Tucson.

Sandra A.

My name is Sandra. I am 49, married with four children, and I'm from Boston. For 33 years I have struggled with an eating disorder, bulimia and anorexia. I have also had a problem with drinking and drugging to numb my feelings....

I knew I was going down in a bad way a few years ago. I had hit rock bottom. I wanted to die. I remember telling God to take me because I couldn't live like this anymore.

I know it was through the grace of God that I was led to Sierra Tucson. I had never been in rehab before, but knew I had to do it or I would surely die. That was the third best decision I had made in my life (besides marrying my husband and being a mother to four beautiful children). Sierra Tucson changed my life; it began my recovery. The only bad thing about it for me was that I was so far away from my family. I was so homesick. Yet, as I look back today, it was the best place for me to be.

I was excited to come home. I wasn't thinking about the things that would be hard for me. After the excitement of being home faded, I knew if I didn't continue this recovery process, I may not be able stay on the path of recovery. The first 48 hours were very strange for me. I didn't realize how hard it was going to be, to be back in a place where I wasn't surrounded by people who understood me without judgment. I started to feel alone and fearful. Thankfully, I had come home with a toolbox that Sierra Tucson gave me while I was there. I knew I couldn't continue to rely on myself. I found an intensive outpatient program where I continued my recovery.

It is two years later. I am sober. I have put on some weight and attend Alcoholics Anonymous meetings every day. I know that I am an alcoholic who suffers with an eating disorder, but as long as I remain in recovery and continue to do the work, I will get better. Today, I am in such a better place than two years ago. I am happy, willing, hopeful and able to ask for help.

Thank you, Sierra Tucson, all the staff, alumni workshops and the people who were there with me. I never could have done it alone.

Rob L.

When I arrived at Sierra Tucson, I was high, very high—too high. That evening, I ended up in an emergency room cardiac unit. As the medical staff got my heart issues under control, the ER doctor explained to me that if I had not gone into rehab, I would have been dead within 45 days....

I knew my life was out of control. I had hit bottom. My life had to change.

The first week at Sierra Tucson, I started to understand why I was there. It was amazing how many new best friends I suddenly had. During the second week, I started to hear the therapists. I was learning many things about myself I had never known. Then, the third week was the very difficult: Family Week. I realized I had a lot of baggage to deal with. The fourth week was much better. Then, I was getting out in a couple of days.

The day I left, I walked to the office to check out. Two weeks earlier, I had been counting the days until my release. Now, I was filled with fear and anxiety. Leaving treatment was becoming a reality. The woman who checked me out was the same person who had admitted me. After I signed the paperwork and got my personal items, she told me that she wanted to show me a picture. It was a picture of me, the day I had been admitted. I was shocked. I was looking at someone who was 25 pounds heavier and so high on drugs he couldn't focus for the camera. My eyes looked like they could never heal. Not only did I feel different from the man who had been admitted to Sierra Tucson four weeks earlier, I looked different. I was a completely different person. Looking at that photo, I actually smiled and laughed. I felt happy. Something I hadn't felt in years. I never wanted to see that person from 30 days earlier again. I wiped the tears from my eyes and gave the woman a big hug, thanked her for showing me the picture, and headed for the door.

When I walked out, I saw my girlfriend sitting in a chair by the fountain at the main entrance. We embraced. It felt so good. I realized I had not seen her with sober eyes for years. She was beautiful, and I knew she was a safe person for me.

During the drive back home to Phoenix, I realized I had a whole new awareness of my surroundings. My brain had been dulled for so long by drugs. Everything I was seeing now seemed new. When we got close to home we stopped at a store to buy groceries. I walked into the store and felt overwhelmed by the activity, music, and sounds. I turned and went back to the car. I realized that reentry was going to take a lot more time.

Upon leaving Sierra Tucson, I was aware pills would be at my house. I planned to find them and get rid of them as soon as I got home. We spent the first several hours searching for pills. Every time we found some, I let my girlfriend take them and throw them in the toilet. I didn't even want to touch them. As we searched, I realized that my fear of running out of drugs must have been huge. We found pills hidden in multiple locations. I continued to find pills from time to time over the next few years.

The first morning out of Sierra Tucson, I followed the advice of the transition class. I set meetings with a therapist and my psychiatrist for the following week. I made a call to get directions and some understanding of the local Sierra Tucson Alumni Support Group. I had been advised to take some time before returning to work. We were leaving in a few hours for a planned trip to Colorado. We were staying at a hotel that I knew, which provided the next entry step for me, and safety.

When I left Sierra Tucson, I had toolbox, a lot of gratitude, willingness, love and hope. I knew I had a huge mess to fix—family issues, self-love issues and staying straight. I knew I couldn't fix everything today. My therapist had advised me to take care of myself first, then the world around me would change.

I am an alcoholic and a drug addict for life. I have been sober since I left Sierra Tucson nine and a half years ago. I continue to take care of myself, and the world around me has changed significantly.

Julie M.

I stayed at Sierra Tucson for six weeks, dealing with alcoholism and trauma. It was finally time for me to go. The staff had printed a list of the Alcoholics Anonymous meetings in my hometown and given me the name of a good trauma therapist, and I had a notebook full of information that I had written and gathered during my treatment. I was afraid to leave; I remember that clearly....

I knew it would be challenging to walk right back into the environment in which I had been drinking before I came. But I knew that the time had come. I had to go.

I remember the van taking me past the "You Are a Miracle" sign that had baffled me when I had arrived. I was beginning to get a glimmer now of what that sign really meant. The tears welled up as I remembered how thoroughly beaten, hopeless, and despairing I had been six weeks before. I felt grateful to Sierra Tucson.

Could I make it all the way home on the airplane without drinking alcohol? Was I going to be able to handle myself in the outside world without a drink? I knew it would be difficult, but I had to try.

I did not feel tempted to drink during that flight, and when I saw my husband (now ex-husband) at the airport, I noticed for the first time how much progress I had made in six weeks. I felt different—a little more self-assured and grounded—and I felt what I now know to be the beginning of true self-esteem. I believe my then-husband commented on how different I seemed.

It was evening, so we went right home. I was afraid to even walk into the den, where I had done most of my drinking. I acted as if the room did not exist. I unpacked and tried to sleep in our bedroom. No such luck. I stayed out in the living room and read until it was time to go to a meeting.

One of the last things a Sierra Tucson therapist said to me before I left was that I must get to an AA meeting as soon as I got home and that I must ask the people there for help. I was never very good at asking for help, but I had practiced a little at Sierra Tucson, and I was scared enough of relapsing that I went to a meeting early the next morning to do just that.

The meeting was at a local AA clubhouse, and I forced myself to walk in and sit at one of the tables. I picked a corner table where there were mostly women. I remember being so scared that I poured my heart out to those at that table, explaining that I had just returned home from treatment and how I was advised to attend a meeting, as soon as possible, and ask for help, which was why I was there. They were very kind, surrounding me with encouragement and understanding. They gave me a list of names and phone numbers that I could call for support. I left, feeling a lot less scared.

I did, however, notice some of my old attitudes bubbling up—resentment, cynicism, and what I now understand to be self-will. The only thing I knew to do about it was to just keep going to meetings. So I did that. I went to a meeting that same evening, and two meetings again the next day. I asked one of the women who had been at that first table to be my sponsor. She agreed, and upon her suggestion I purchased AA's "Big Book."

I will have seven years of sobriety in a few weeks, and I consider that to be a miracle. Now I really do understand the "You Are a Miracle" sign at Sierra Tucson's front gates.

The one thing I would say about my recovery is that I couldn't possibly have known seven years ago that I would feel the way I do today or that my life would look like it does now. I have come to understand that what God has in store for me is far, far greater than anything I can possibly imagine in the present moment. It is my job to stay sober and let Him work with me.

Thank you, Sierra Tucson, for giving me such a good start. I am forever grateful.

Ashley K.

I completed 30 days at Sierra Tucson. I was free to go, except for one problem: I was positively petrified!

I procrastinated. I wanted to say goodbye to every single person who meant anything to me during my stay; that was clearly an impossible task when some of the beautiful souls I'd met during my time there were long gone....

In vain, I was attempting to prevent the inevitable—leaving the cocoon, the safe haven, the desert oasis.

I remember feeling mostly terrified that I was the only one responsible for myself; I had no one else to hold me accountable. Did I really have that level of authority? I just didn't think so! I was absolutely horrified that I would run toward, and go through, every single fast-food restaurant from Tucson to Phoenix, literally devouring every solitary food item I craved, wanted, and fantasized about during my 30 days at Sierra Tucson. To my surprise, and despite my utter lack of confidence, that didn't happen. As the miles passed beneath the wheels of my car, I felt my confidence grow. I managed to find my way home, and even remembered how to find my way to the clinic where I had dropped off my cat 90 days earlier.

The weekend loomed before me as I walked into my apartment with my cat in her carrier. I was still feeling exceptionally intimidated and I had an overwhelming thought: What – Do – I – Do – Now?

My very structured schedule of places to be at specific times at Sierra Tucson had vanished and I was all alone, now responsible once more for myself and my cat. I came home, and although the specifics of that time now elude me, I do remember I was frantic to find a recovery meeting, knowing my Adult Children of Alcoholics meeting was still five days away.

I decided the healthiest thing for me to do was to pick up the phone and let my loved ones know that I was home safe. I reached out to a good friend of mine who lived fairly close. She was, and still is, a "safe" friend who I knew would not want to celebrate my homecoming by going to a favorite restaurant.

We went to the mall and I felt exceedingly overwhelmed by the visual stimulation and buzzing energy within its walls.

It was as if I had landed on another planet; I struggled to stay present in my body. I tried to explain to my friend where I had been, what I had experienced, and what I had learned, but sadly, it was as if I were speaking a foreign language. She had no affiliation with addiction or recovery. All I could think about was, "Who would understand my point of view?"

So, I researched various 12-Step meetings in the Phoenix area and found a few I could try, one of which was Emotions Anonymous. Unfortunately, it was on the opposite side of town, a good hour drive each way, with an hour meeting in the middle, and that worried me. What if discussing my emotions was triggering? It turned out that I did not like that meeting, but I kept my commitment to go at least three times before concluding it was not a good match. A few other options that I thought might work, but eventually eliminated, were Co-Dependents Anonymous and Overeaters Anonymous. After so many meetings with different rhythms and traditions, my brain felt more like a bowl of scrambled eggs or whipped potatoes!

I took the time to talk over my bewilderment after discussing my very anxious dilemma with a confidant at my Adult Children of Alcoholics meeting. It was then that I decided that ACoA was a solid fit and, indeed, was enough for me. I left Sierra Tucson with a step-by-step plan of how to continue taking care of myself as I did while I was there. About a week after discharge, I attended my new intensive outpatient program. I struggled with the "perfection picture" I had created, especially because I was in a different reality at the IOP. I was naïve as to how hard it would be to follow my plan in this new environment, since the Sierra Tucson "bubble" was an entirely safe place to grow and share, and the rules were very different in the real world.

Binge eating disorder resources have come a long way since the time I sought help after leaving Sierra Tucson. At the time, I was unable to find a solid obesity IOP, so I had to piece things together myself. Because I had found one that didn't specialize in eating disorders, I knew I would be faced with taking care of my emotional and mental health.

I hunkered down in my house. I did domestic chores that occupied my time and helped me not feel so untethered. I called my older sister. I secured my Sierra Tucson meal card to the front of my fridge. I went shopping. I bought food, and I promptly and diligently portioned out the appropriate amounts so I could continue the comfortable and familiar routine of eating within my meal plan.

It was not the same, but I had the tools and I worked the tools. I wrote in my journal and I bought self-care cards. I eventually developed a morning routine of lighting a candle, drawing a card, and focusing on words like gratitude, serenity, mindfulness, and patience.

As my anxiety ebbed and flowed, I found myself taking life one day at a time, sometimes even hour by hour. The road of recovery is not paved with ease, or gold, or even perfection. But what I have found is that no matter what obstacles, hurdles, or potholes I encounter, the tools I acquired at Sierra Tucson have helped me find my way and understand myself better. And for that, I am forever thankful, hopeful, and blessed.

Gus C.

I remember little of the day I left Sierra Tucson and my first day home. I do, however, clearly recall seeing the sign that read "You Are a Miracle" on the way out of the Sierra Tucson driveway. At that moment, I remembered that the sign read "Expect a Miracle" on the way in....

Although nothing miraculous hit me, I do recall realizing I was alive, clean, and sober, and feeling OK. Being alive, let alone clean and sober for more than one month, was not something I had expected from the way I previously drank and used drugs. And that "OK" feeling was a combination of shame and anxiety, mixed with hope and a tinge of confidence—not so much in myself, but that things could be all right. Those unfamiliar feelings of hope and confidence were a result of my stay at Sierra Tucson.

Still, I was not sure how I was going to do this sobriety thing. I was told I had to change all of the people, places, things, and situations associated with my addiction. But since I drank alcohol and used drugs at home, at work, in the car between home and work, and everywhere else I went, and I had isolated myself from almost everyone during the last few years of active addiction, I realized the only way to do this was to change me. So, how to change me became the challenge.

Sierra Tucson had been a great experience, thanks to my primary therapist, the fellowship and friendships, the location, and the scenery. But I knew this was not real life—at least not my real life. I was quite anxious as the day of discharge approached, so I asked a therapist two days before discharge how I was supposed to do this sobriety thing away from the protection of Sierra Tucson. He said (and I think he was appealing to my rational-scientific mind), "Those who have the greatest chance of being clean and sober at one year from leaving Sierra Tucson do four things: attend 90 recovery meetings in 90 days; get a home group as soon as possible; get a sponsor, at least a temporary one, within seven days; and most importantly, get to a recovery meeting within 24 hours of arriving home."

For reasons I was not aware of at the time, I took his words to heart. I wasn't sure about the 90 meetings in 90 days or the sponsor, since it was all so new to me. But getting to a meeting right away was something that I felt I could do, and that provided just enough hope and confidence to motivate me. Eventually, I came to understand that the reason I took the therapist's advice was that I trusted him and his intention to be of service. Now, I actually don't remember too much about him. All I can recall was that he was not an MD, a PhD, or a high-ranking staff member. He was simply another addict in recovery working as a nighttime therapist who was trying to help by connecting with me.

Upon returning home, I went to a local recovery meeting about 24 hours later. I was confused and anxious yet hopeful, as I was simply being present with fellow addicts and alcoholics who were doing this sobriety thing with nothing to sell, no expectations, no preaching, no demands—just a bunch of us trying to stay sober and help each other achieve sobriety. I don't remember anything about the meeting except the clubhouse, a place where I still attend recovery meetings. I did attend another meeting the next day, and eventually—and to my surprise—I went to 120 meetings in 90 days, got a sponsor within a week, and established myself in two home groups.

I have fond memories of my stay at Sierra Tucson. And even though I never connected with anyone who was there at the same time I was, I still owe a lot to my fellow residents, the staff, the doctors, and the therapists. It's where my recovery started, and where my life restarted.

I have such gratitude! It used to be that everything that killed me made me feel alive. Now, it's different. It is everything that reminds me that someday there will be a last moment that deepens my gratitude for this very moment. And at this moment, I'm grateful to be alive—without the things that were once killing me.

Lilia G.

Every morning when I was at Sierra Tucson, I dutifully completed a feelings form. But on my last morning in Tucson, I could barely distinguish between all of the feelings and emotions swirling inside of me. Eager, scared, excited, terrified, my heart beating, my hands shaking, I walked out to the parking lot to the car that would take me to the airport....

As we cruised down the highway, the driver asked, "So, are you better? What were you doing there? How long have you been there?"

I was shocked. I knew, though, that I could handle the questions with grace. "Two months," I answered, "and I'm working on it."

The airport was a blur. I had been cocooned in one world for two months, and prior to that, in a hospital without outdoor access for a little over two weeks. I looked around in a daze at people walking briskly to their gates, tapping away at their phones, and gulping Starbucks. I had forgotten what it felt like to be free. The sentiment of being trapped in treatment had crept up on me in the past week, and I saw it as a sign that I was ready to leave. I took a deep breath. I was prepared. I was ready. I could do this.

Then, on my layover, I began to think. I wasn't losing my desire to remain in recovery, no, but I was slowly pondering what it would feel like to do the harmful behaviors that had landed me in treatment in the first place. What would it feel like to cut? To purge? To stop taking my medication? I looked down at the three containers I was clutching in my lap; the containers held my meals and snacks for the day. It dawned on me that I didn't have to eat them if I didn't want to. I threw them away.

By the time I got home that night, I felt free. I was alone in my apartment and had an entire day before I was to meet my parents for a weeklong family trip. I could do anything I wanted. So I ordered food. I ate it. I purged. I ate some more. I purged again. Repeat, repeat, repeat. I fell asleep in the bathroom. I woke up in the middle of the night, exhausted. "Fuck it," I thought to myself. I went to self-harm, but then

I paused. I wanted to do it, but there was a block. I couldn't. I crumpled on the hard tile floor of the bathroom and cried.

As the sun came up, I knew what I had to do. I remembered everything I had worked on at Sierra Tucson. I remembered what it was like earlier, in the hospital. I remembered my suicide attempt. I remembered everything that led to it, and knew that I was no longer that girl. I had grown. I was different. "I am a miracle," I thought to myself, and grinned. I thought it was cheesy, but knew it to be true.

Determined to make this day better than the last, I opened a new journal and wrote a gratitude list. Writing a daily list was a practice I had begun at Sierra Tucson—every day. It allowed me to realize the gifts I had been given in this life. I glanced beside me on my desk at my gold graduation coin emblazoned with the Serenity Prayer. I picked up my pen and began.

- I am grateful for my body, for the sacred structure that allows me to move and feel and touch and smell and taste and hear.

- I am grateful for my mind, for my desire and willingness to continue on the path of recovery, for the compassion I am able to have for myself at this very moment.

- I am alive, and for that, I am grateful.

I recognized that a lapse was not a relapse, that I had the tools and the power to continue healing. And I was worthy of being healed. I was worthy of love.

Joshua G.

When planning my departure from Sierra Tucson, I made sure that I left after the Burning Ceremony. I had one last letter to my former self, one last list of regrets and resentments, to let go of before I could reenter the world....

Nothing seemed the same about me, although I am sure the more observant friend or family member would have found many attributes of my personality unshaken.

As I said goodbye to the friends who had become my family in the lobby of the lodge where I had resided during my stay, I had a vague desire to go back to Day One and start all over. I wondered, "Is there an option for a lifetime rehab program? Can I just vent my feelings in a safe process group for the rest of my life?" That, however, was not an option. As I left and went out to the Sierra Tucson parking lot, and into the arms of my eager family, I had no idea what to expect. While I had found placement next in an extended care program, which was a marvelous opportunity, that itself was another mystery.

As we drove from Tucson to Phoenix, the stars seemed intimidating. Anxiety attacked me—the fear of who, what, where, when, why did I agree to go on this treatment path anyway? Can't I just go back to the days when my greatest worry was whether or not I could sleep in in the morning? Everything was out of my control, and for a codependent-alcoholic-depressive like me, even admitting something was out of my control was a terrifying prospect.

As the Santa Catalina Mountains passed by in the dark, I focused on my breathing and chanted the Serenity Prayer until the anxiety eased. When we got home, I was taking out my suitcases when I realized that I had left my backpack—ID, wallet, and plane tickets to California, EVERYTHING—in the lobby of the lodge at Sierra Tucson. Whether it was a subconscious desire to stay behind or just an unfortunate mishap, my father and I made the turnaround trip back to Tucson.

Several roadblocks and seven hours later, I collapsed onto the guest bed of my parents' house for an hour of sleep before my flight. I think the only thing that kept alcohol off of my mind was pure exhaustion. The airport proved to be a hub of temptation, but all I wanted was more sleep. I moved past the bars and wine lounges to my gate, curled up, and slept in the middle of the airport. If there was one thing Sierra Tucson had taught me, it was to take care of self before worrying about the judgment of others.

After another stint of traveling, I found myself at my extended care program, specifically designed for men, ages 20–30, struggling with addiction. It felt right and I was immediately welcomed into the community. Activity filled my first day—group therapy, psychiatry appointments, and grocery shopping. In the evening, I found myself near Seal Beach, California, for a speaker meeting. Still wanting nothing but a nap, I remember being blown away by the number of people filling the baby blue-painted building. There were hundreds of men and women waiting for a speaker—hundreds of people like me.

I sat on the floor near other young recovering alcoholics and addicts and I didn't feel afraid anymore. I don't remember the speaker's name or many of the nuances of his or her talk. But I do remember the sense of belonging I felt. For the next hour and a half, while the speaker talked, I found my anxiety drifting away. For the first time I discovered the magic of Alcoholics Anonymous—that through sharing our stories and identifying with another person's wounds, we could find healing within ourselves.

As my first 48 hours out of treatment drew to a close, that sense of belonging soon became the makings of self-worth. With self-worth came the courage to undertake the 12 Steps with the same fervor I had when approaching a bottle of liquor. As the days slipped by, I found the gifts of the program, and more importantly, I discovered the beautiful miracles within my own skin—the perfect imperfection of my new self. ▨

Tiffany S.

Sierra Tucson was my first attempt at recovery and, thankfully, my last. It was the first time I could completely melt, unravel, and fall apart. Most of the moments before leaving Sierra Tucson are fuzzy, at best, but what I do remember very clearly is the fear. The intense, heightened anxiety and the paralyzing fear....

What if I didn't make it? What if I was one of the many who relapsed, who screwed up, who wasted the money and the time spent at Sierra Tucson? I had absolutely no idea how I was going to maintain my recovery past the safe structure of Sierra Tucson, and I was aware that the odds were highly unfavorable. What I did know was how to take and follow direction, even if I wasn't sure it would work.

The direction I was given was to "go to aftercare" (whatever that meant?). I was told that going back home, where my sickness was born and had festered, was a really bad idea. Staff told me that going to another facility after Sierra Tucson was a much better idea. I selected my next destination. It seemed really straightforward, but I was terrified of leaving the safety of Sierra Tucson. I didn't know how to do anything sober. I asked to have someone travel with me. I felt like a little kid. I figured if I could just stay at Sierra Tucson forever, then I'd be safe.

I remember arriving at the airport with a random staff person I didn't even know. I was still rough around the edges and most certainly needed an attitude adjustment, especially when I was scared. I was snarky with my travel companion as she guided me through the maze of airport objects and people, rolling my eyes, and telling her I didn't need help. Then we arrived at the front of the security line and they told me I was going to get patted down! I had just spent the month being respectfully asked if I could accept a handshake, a tap on the shoulder, a hug. Now this reckless stranger was going to touch me, without permission, on my body?

I felt like a raw nerve and, suddenly, I was very grateful for my travel companion, all snarkiness aside. As the airport security patted me down, I felt violated. I started to cry. I was embarrassed to be seen crying in front of people who didn't say "we support you" and told me that I was Sierra Tucson "safe." I was not safe. I did not feel supported. I wanted to crawl back into the pot-hazed, pill-induced hole I had crawled out of 28 days prior. I somehow made it onto the plane, travel companion in tow. The rest is hazy until I arrived at my next treatment destination.

When I arrived at the next place, my entitlement issues came into play. Sierra Tucson was so pristine; I was spoiled. I was sorely disappointed when I arrived at my continuing care facility. It was "rustic," there weren't as many amenities, but mostly, I was just uncomfortable in my skin. I called my mom from the laundry area to cry and complain. I didn't know these weird people; I had just left my safe cocoon; and I definitely did not want to stay where I was—they did it all wrong! Thankfully, Mom knew how to soothe me in that moment and persuaded me to stay long enough to give it a chance.

Leaving Sierra Tucson, I realized, was not a graduation so much but rather the beginning of this new life I was forging called recovery. That first night out, and many nights thereafter, I sat on the comfiest couch ever. I snuggled in a warm blanket, ate freshly popped popcorn, and watched Law & Order: SVU with my new community. They were really nice, and, just like me, they also were scared and unsure.

Little did I know that those first 48 hours were the first of a series that would bring me to more than 11 years in recovery not only from drug and alcohol addiction but also from the plethora of other "titles" I had earned at Sierra Tucson. I am Tiffany and today, I am a thriving addict, codependent, eating-disordered trauma survivor who is grateful for every 48 hours I am given. Turns out I did beat those odds after all!

Shannon S.

I went to Sierra Tucson twice—once for anorexia and the second time for alcohol.

When I went the first time, I was kicking and screaming. I only went because my boyfriend insisted I go. He had gone to Sierra Tucson previously, and I had been to Family Week when he was there, so I was familiar with it, but I certainly didn't want to go for myself and deal with my issues....

I was scared to death—after all, the one thing I had control over in my life was my eating. I could control how thin I was. I cried going there, and I remember crying a lot while I was there. I was terrified of gaining weight.

The second time I went, however, was quite different. I wanted to go. I really wanted to go because I knew I needed help. After my first experience, which turned out well and basically saved my life, Sierra Tucson became such a special place for me. This time heading into treatment, I was struggling with something different: alcohol. I knew it was where I needed to go. Yet, I didn't know how I was going to make it happen. I was pretty sure my insurance would not cover it. Then, one day after a horrific binge episode the night before, I got a call from my mom: "I have been on the phone with Sierra Tucson. Your husband, Dad and I are going to make it happen. You are going back." I remember I was driving and I had to pull over because I started to cry. I was so grateful to be going back. I knew I was going to be in a safe place. I knew there was hope.

Leaving after 30 days of treatment was sad. A few days before leaving, I began thinking that although I was ready to go, I knew saying goodbye to the wonderful people I had met and the new friends I had made would be hard. I wondered if I would ever see them again. There was so much hugging and so many tears—streams and streams of tears. You get so close and you learn so much about each other. Leaving was like an emotional hangover. And compounding my sadness was that I wasn't certain what I would face when I got back home to New Jersey. My husband and I were not in a good place, and I wasn't sure if I was going to stay married or that I even wanted to stay married.

The car service took me to Tucson International Airport the day of my departure. I remember being quiet during the ride there. The sadness hung over me like a low-level cloud. I remember looking at the mountains and feeling gratitude that I had been able to go to treatment there. Driving away I made a goal for myself to return to the annual Sierra Tucson Alumni Retreat, which I attended that year and have been back nearly every year since.

This time going to the airport, I knew I wouldn't drink. I didn't want to get off the plane bombed. For me the airport and the plane always involved alcohol. This would be the first time at the airport or on the plane without it. I amused myself by watching everyone. There were so many people at the bar and so many people who were getting drinks on the plane. I started counting the number of drinks they would have. I remember thinking that this person had this many and this person had that many, and deciding that they were probably alcoholics.

But then I began to immerse myself in the books I had gotten from Sierra Tucson, reading the activities I had participated in, and just reviewing the work we had covered—all the positive work! In that way I kept Sierra Tucson close to me during the entire flight home. I had my affirmation books and my Daily Reflections book by Alcoholics Anonymous. I just kept looking at it to see what it said. I also wrote in my journal. Those tools got me home.

My husband was there to pick me up when I arrived; I was excited to see him and he was excited to see me. But I was still feeling fearful as I know he was. We had missed each other, but we both knew we had work to do. I had seen my husband during my stay because he had come for Family Week, so he knew some of what had transpired there. Yet, I remember being angry with him when he picked me up because he didn't ask me anything about my experience. There were so many wonderful things that happened and I felt that he didn't care. I think we were still angry at each other for everything that had happened previously between us.

The next day my husband went to work and I went to a recovery meeting. (My goal was 90 meetings in 90 days and I did it!) It was a new meeting and I chose to share. I was excited to be there because although I had been to meetings before, I knew now that I was looking healthier after completing treatment. But I also knew down deep that I was still proceeding on my self-will and not fully using the tools I had learned at Sierra Tucson. I wasn't ready to completely let go as evidenced by the fact that people would ask me if I had a sponsor yet. I would reply that I was looking, but, in actuality, I wasn't.

I was staying sober, but I was essentially a "dry drunk." After all, the insanity of my self-talk was still there and I had to fight it. I remember thinking that my husband was having an affair, along with many other delusional thoughts, and I still had horrible anxiety attacks. But somehow I (barely) managed to plow through them. I went to meetings; I talked to people; and eventually I went to a new therapist. She was perfect for me. She had years of sobriety and knew about eating disorders and understood everything that was going on. My husband and I went to her together, as well as separately, for a long time. She really helped.

There was so much to work on—my marriage and myself. And then after a horrific relapse that almost killed me, I remember saying, "I am so done. I will do whatever it takes!" I finally got a sponsor. I was sick and tired of being sick and tired. I wasn't drinking to get drunk at this point. I was drinking to get rid of my awful anxiety and panic attacks. I called someone who had a lot of time in the program and asked her to please help me and that I would do whatever I needed to do. And that's when the miracles started happening.

I got my sponsor the day after I relapsed. She took me through AA's "Big Book," and I remember when she read the AA Promises. She said if you work these Steps and follow directions, these will come true for you. "Are you sure?" I asked.

"Yes, I promise the Promises will come true," she said. "Just go through the Steps and they will happen." I needed reassurance. I wanted to be sure.

And today I am sure. I lead such a different life now and I live with such gratitude. I am an aesthetician, and prior to going to Sierra Tucson, I worked at a salon. But when I came back, I knew I couldn't be there anymore. It was not a healthy environment for me. I recognized the need to own my own business and make my own schedule. So I began working out of my house. It turns out that I love my home business because it gives me control and allows me the flexibility to go to meetings and do what I need to do to support my recovery.

Going to Sierra Tucson helped me to recognize that I needed to look at all areas of my life, including my job and my marriage. I realized I needed support, because I couldn't do it on my own without a sponsor. Before I got my sponsor and leading up to my relapse, I was literally dropping to my knees in desperation asking God for help. Out of the relapse, I had the motivation to get a sponsor. She helped me to see that working the Steps would work for me. And it did. I went from this feeling of doom-and-gloom and nearly getting a divorce to working the Steps and feeling happy, joyous, and free. Miracles happened when I worked the Steps! It totally transformed me and saved my marriage. Today I go to several meetings a week, have an awesome sponsor, and am finally comfortable in my own skin.

It really is unbelievable how transformation happens once you let go of self-will, follow directions, and do the work. I am so unbelievably grateful. I am a miracle.

Garrett B.

After spending six weeks at Sierra Tucson, I was on my way to the next step in my recovery journey. I was now faced with the world I had left behind when I walked through the doors of Sierra Tucson, and my emotions were mixed with utter excitement and even more uncertainty of the road ahead…

At the airport, I walked past a busy bar and was quickly reminded of the world I left behind weeks prior. That world had not changed one bit. The positive in this reality was that I had changed; my experience and stay at Sierra Tucson had gifted me with enough strength to walk by that airport bar and straight to my gate—a feat I had not accomplished for seven years or so. That airplane flew me to Newport Beach, California, where I was to spend the next two months in extended care treatment for drug and alcohol addiction.

At Sierra Tucson, there was a warm blanket of support and care, and the openness of the people was contagious; I found many new challenges adapting to my new location. I thought back on the invaluable lessons that I had learned during my first day after leaving Sierra Tucson—that you need to stick with the winners who value recovery and health.

Although my first 48 hours were nerve-racking, stemming from all the unknowns ahead, the metamorphosis that had occurred in six short weeks at Sierra Tucson gifted me with the tools and strength needed to grow in situations of immediate turmoil, and I am forever grateful. I consider myself lucky, for endless reasons, but mostly for having the opportunity of recovery and continuing to follow that gifted road today, five and a half years later. The world in which I live will always have challenges that I must face. In recovery, I am allowed the ability to face these challenges and grow to my full potential, from the first day, and forever after, if I choose so.

Sara D.

I was nervous, scared, hopeful, guarded. My husband, Lance, was picking me up. This would be the first time we would see each other since Family Week. A lot happened at Family Week that we needed to go over....

I was the last of my process group to leave, and most of my friends that I made had left within the past five days. I had packed my suitcases and rolled them out to the doors that brought me into Sierra Tucson. I looked to my right and saw the office where I completed my intake papers and placed my phone, my wallet, and my identity. It looked so much smaller now. Just a room.

My husband was waiting in the lobby, smiling nervously and looking supportive. We walked out to the car, and as I got in, he handed me an envelope. I opened it, not sure what I would find.

Life's Pathway

An Inspirational Message by Emily Matthews

At times, life's path seems filled
with things that make the going rough,

And we wish there were a smoother road,
for we feel we've had enough...

But, if we pause a moment
and remember Who's in charge,

The hills that loom ahead of
us no longer seem so large.

And every rock before us,
when we know we're not alone,

Becomes, not just a stumbling block,
but one more stepping stone.

Of course, I cried. Our marriage was on very shaky ground, and he was showing me that we had hope.

Driving home was so strange. For the past 30 days I had only moved as fast as my feet could take me. Now, I was hurtling home at 55 miles per hour with the landscape whizzing past me. It was surreal and overwhelming. I tried to focus on the road in front of me and the conversation with Lance.

Lance brought me back home and had to go back to work. Before he left, he asked me just to take my time going through the house, into each room, and try to scrub out any negativity and find peace. There were a lot of memories, fights, tears, and flashbacks in that house before I left for Sierra Tucson.

Leaving Sierra Tucson, where I had learned to feel safe most of the time, meant leaving my "bubble." I had to find a way to create that safety back at home. I walked through each room, looking around, trying to feel something. I really was too anxious to feel much, though. This place felt familiar and foreign all at once.

I pulled out my sign-in book from Sierra Tucson and started calling my friends to let them know I was home and to check in with them. It felt good to talk to people who understood the strangeness of returning home and reconnecting with them about the events of the past few days since they had left.

Reconnecting with my Sierra Tucson peeps was one of the most valuable actions I took that first day. It brought me comfort, grounded me, and helped me know I was not alone. They were my touch point to know that my time at Sierra Tucson was real.

The first night's dinner was a challenge for me. I love to cook but was afraid to even try cooking at first. I was certain I would forget something on the stove or not be able to keep up with the basic steps of the process of putting together a meal. I didn't want to go out because I was afraid there would be too much sound and movement, too many people and decisions. We just ordered in that first night.

The first night, when I couldn't sleep, I went out and turned on the TV. This was my usual pattern to get my brain focused on something other than my bad dreams. I was shocked when the screen flashed by so fast that it was jarring and uncomfortable. Commercials especially were too much to take, so I would put my hands over my eyes until they were over. (Many commercials still bother me because of the quick jump from image to image!) I remember finding an old black-and-white movie that I could focus on. The people spoke slower, images moved slower, and I wasn't bothered by too much visual input.

The next day I pulled out my Sierra Tucson folder with my continuing care instructions. I read through the schedule I planned for myself, as well as the list of suggested resources to look up. I was full of hope and determined that I was going to "do this right" by throwing myself into my recovery program. The schedule I set was that, while I was still taking time off work, I would make my recovery my full-time job. My logic was that while at Sierra Tucson, I worked about 40 hours a week on active recovery activities. It made sense to continue this over the next month until I started working again. My initial list included:

- **See my regular therapist.** I had a scheduled appointment already and planned to schedule weekly appointments for the next month.

- **Read.** I brought home a bunch of books from Sierra Tucson that I had not yet read. One of them was Waking the Tiger: Healing Trauma by Peter Levine, and I had a CD with exercises to go along with the book. I wanted to read through the book and work on the exercises daily.

- **Art therapy.** I enjoyed drawing mandalas and using art to express my feelings while I was at Sierra Tucson, so I planned to continue adding this to my weekly schedule.

- **Meetings.** I had to find meetings for Adult Children of Alcoholics, Co-Dependents Anonymous, an incest survivors or trauma survivors group, and a PTSD support group. I was also planning on going to the local Sierra Tucson Alumni Support Group.

- **Find a Somatic Experiencing Practitioner**

- **Meditate**

- **Journal**

To be honest, finding meetings and therapists was difficult for me. I would try to search online and couldn't make sense of all the information that was being shown. My brain felt mushy, and my focus and concentration were limited in this capacity.

The highlight of Day Two was receiving a call from the Sierra Tucson alumni coordinator. He was checking in to see how I was doing and what I needed help with and to offer support. It was so nice to have someone from Sierra Tucson following up and making sure I knew I was now a part of a larger community that cared about my journey and was there to support me through it. He provided me with names and numbers of local resources and provided the contact information for my local Sierra Tucson Alumni Support Group.

Later that day I saw my regular therapist and shared with her some of the highlights of my time at Sierra Tucson and scheduled appointments for the next few weeks.

Overall, my first 48 hours out of Sierra Tucson was full of surprises. I didn't know what to expect. I was overwhelmed with sensory input, received amazing gifts of love and support, and was finding out that I was experiencing the world around me differently than I did before I went in. I felt like an alien and was going to have to learn how to use the tools from my time at Sierra Tucson to develop a new way of living.

And it was worth it.

Matt E.

I was riddled with every emotion under the sun upon leaving Sierra Tucson, but the emotions I remember most were fear and excitement. Walking out of Sierra Tucson, I thought back on the many memorable moments I had there: the first night when I actually slept a full night for the first time in over a year; being weaned off medications; the exhaustion I felt after Family Week; my first true laugh in what felt like forever; and finally feeling like myself again. I was nervous to leave the "bubble," to say the least....

I don't remember the Tucson airport. But I do remember connecting in Atlanta and changing terminals, passing the bar where I was boozing heavily on the layover while on my way to Sierra Tucson. It threw me for a loop. Something inside me told me to go back in; no one would know. I thought about how I felt at that moment versus how I had felt 30 days before and sped up my walk to the other terminal.

I did not fly directly home. My wife was in another state to pick the kids up from camp, so I flew there to meet her. She had come for Family Week, and it was an incredibly stressful week for both of us. Our marriage was definitely in flux. She looked exhausted, and feelings of guilt and shame crept in immediately. I just remember telling myself to breathe. This was not going to be easy.

I felt incredibly uneasy on the three-hour drive to the mountains to pick up the kids. The conversation was forced and tense, and all I wanted to do was snap my fingers and get back to Sierra Tucson. I didn't know if I was ready to apply what I had learned in Arizona in the real world. I tried to remind myself that this was a process and that 15 years of lies, resentments and distrust were not going to disappear overnight. "Breathe, Matt, breathe. You have to move forward. This is not going to be a cakewalk," I told myself.

After what felt like an interminable trip, we arrived at camp to get the kids. What a wonderful distraction! I felt immense joy when I saw them and teared up immediately. This was the first of many overwhelmingly emotional moments I would come to experience in the near term. I had not cried for 10 years (yes, 10 years!) before Sierra Tucson. The spigot opened at a therapy session at Sierra Tucson and I found myself having a hard time turning it off! It felt good, although I could tell the kids were like, "What's up with Dad?"

After we arrived at the hotel down the road from camp, my wife asked me to go back to the car to get something she mistakenly left behind. On the way back into the lobby a big television showed an important swimming race in the 2012 Summer Olympics. I sat there and watched, then headed back to the room. My wife met me at the door and accosted me. "Where were you? Why'd it take so long? Did you call someone?" she asked. I felt panicked even though I had done nothing wrong—this was going to be a long road. I remembered what was written on my therapist's board: Trust = Healthy Behavior + Time. Time's going to take some time.

The only thing I remember about the second 48 hours was that I received two phone calls. The first was from my boss (who had tried to dissuade me from going to rehab), who said the human resources department had called him to make sure I was going to be back at work Monday. I thought he and I had already discussed that my first day back would be Wednesday. Ugh, ugh, ugh. Welcome back to the real world!

The other call I received was right before we went to bed. My cell phone rang. I didn't recognize the number. In what would be a poor decision, I answered the call. It was a stripper whom I had spent a ridiculous amount of money on the week before I left for Sierra Tucson. "Do you want to go out and party?" she asked.

"Hey, I'm sure it will all get better. Keep praying," I replied and hung up the phone.

My wife looked at me suspiciously. "Who was that?" she asked.

"A friend from Sierra Tucson who is struggling," I replied and looked away immediately. The lies had begun. It was the first night I did not sleep in over a month.

Maggie A.

(family member)

When I left Family Week at Sierra Tucson, I remember feeling overwhelmed with all the information given to me about my husband's addictions. I felt sadness and betrayal. And I was angry. Yet I also felt a little bit of hope....

I was processing a lot of what had happened during Family Week with my husband, his peers, and his therapist, as well as anything I could from the group I attended. I felt so alone, as if no one understood what I was going through as a family member.

I couldn't help but think, if my husband had the problem, then why was I given discharge instructions to seek recovery for myself? I remember putting them away and thinking, "What the hell? I didn't create this. I don't need Al-Anon. He has the problem; I don't." Included in the discharge instructions was a notebook about boundary setting, including couples therapy and self-care.

When I left Tucson and came back to Dallas, I was eager to tell my family about Family Week. But when I returned, I discovered that they did not understand the power of addiction. In fact, they felt that when he left he would be cured of his addictions and that would be that. Yet, for me, after seeing the Sierra Tucson treatment team and the facility and learning about recovery, my hope was that this addiction was something from which he could recover. Although they didn't completely understand, it helped that I had friends and family with whom I could talk.

I remember feeling overwhelmed and thinking about his recovery and what the future looked like. I was constantly obsessing. I had an Al-Anon book that I purchased during Family Week and I was trying to make sense of that. I also remember reaching out to a Codependents of Sex Addicts member and trying to make sense of the addiction. I remember it being painful. I had so much anguish. I felt like the family dream was broken. I felt lost. Looking back on those first 48 hours, I don't remember what I said or what I did. But I do remember I had bought a T-shirt from the Sierra Tucson bookstore while I was on campus that included the Serenity Prayer. I liked that. I still have that shirt.

It wasn't until Family Week that I got mini-disclosure of the intensity of the addiction so that I could get tested. It was that week that I heard the reality. That was a lot to take. I first heard of Al-Anon that week, but I didn't go until two or three weeks after that, and I haven't stopped going since.

Now I believe in family involvement. The issue does involve family dynamics. In the beginning, I gave them the "evil eye" for the discharge instructions, but the family has to be involved. As family, we play a part. I was grateful to have my eyes opened to that.

Dewey A.

With the completion of Family Week at Sierra Tucson, I was scheduled to leave for home a few days later. My wife planned to visit her family in another city before returning home two days after me. I would be home alone for two days. Could I muster the requisite intestinal fortitude to stay clean until she returned?...

"Yes," I told myself. After all, I shopped with fervor for one of the best substance abuse residential programs I could find. Sierra Tucson's diverse curriculum proved to be what I hoped it would be—no, what I needed it to be. My engaging participation and receptivity enabled me to build a strong platform from which to launch a viable recovery. I had amassed a veritable plethora of weapons to bring to bear on my cunning and baffling enemy.

The stage was set. I would arrive home and be safe for two days. Or would I? Enter Wise Mind. I had lied to me in the past, without even knowing it, telling myself things like: "It will be different this time," "I can use some then put it away," "They won't find out." With repeated failures, I had learned these thoughts were in fact lies, and that I could not trust my Addict Mind. The day may come when I could trust me again, but not yet. For now, vigilance must take the point position through this jungle.

What to do? I knew the answer was within, and I knew how to extract it. I discussed the matter with my Sierra Tucson roommate. I shared my concerns with my wife. It became an open discussion in my group therapy session. I already knew what to do. It was the confirmation, the sounding board I was looking for. I would stay on at Sierra Tucson for two more days and arrive at the airport near our home within two hours of my wife's expected arrival. My first 48 hours out of residential treatment just became my last 48 hours in residential treatment.

Once the decision was made, the flight changed. I advised my appointed consultants, and a great weight was lifted. I had no pressure on me to maintain homeostasis. I had ensured my safety until I arrived home. My hands had seized the reins of my recovery, and confidence was piquing. The hunted had become the hunter. I felt encapsulated in serenity and was heading down a path long since untrodden by my tired feet. My Wise Mind had outsmarted my Addict Mind. This would be the first victorious battle in a war for my life. ▨

Amy B.

Sierra Tucson was a life-changing experience. What was amazing to me was that I had finally found a place where I felt safe, a place where people "got" me, a place where I felt supported, directed, and nurtured (and a place where I actually allowed it). I found hope that healing was possible....

And though I had a plan in place—a sponsor, a home group, a supportive husband, and outside help—leaving Sierra Tucson was like falling off a cliff.

I had no idea what to expect. I was overwhelmed. There was still such a huge gap in the outside world between my experience at Sierra Tucson and my experience outside. Before I left, I had been eager to put into practice the recovery tools I had learned at Sierra Tucson. Yet, once I left, I was terrified.

I didn't know the first thing about handling life on life's terms, or, more importantly, about having patience with myself until I did. No one had told me what they felt like after they left, or what I might feel like. They had just cheered me on, and told me to go to recovery meetings and stick with my plan.

Even though I had spent a month at Sierra Tucson, I thought my feelings were all wrong. I thought I should be able to handle things, should feel better, I should be as capable as others thought I was, I should be further along. I didn't recognize how much I was "should-ing" on myself, rather than asking for help. So I left Sierra Tucson and, once again, my insides didn't match my outsides.

The first week was really difficult. Every day, every hour sometimes, was a struggle. There were no Sierra Tucson continuing care or alumni support groups at that time, and certainly no one who spoke the same Sierra Tucson language, even if they spoke the language of Alcoholics Anonymous. A couple of other residents who attended Sierra Tucson with me were struggling as much as I was. I heard that a couple of people had used alcohol or drugs. I wish I could say that I was not one of them, but I was. It took me a few months to get back into recovery. I was fortunate to have been able to return to Sierra Tucson and complete another 28 days.

Leaving treatment was scary. I thought life after treatment would be easier, and although I just wanted to feel better, I drank again because of my fear. In spite of the very vulnerable way I felt—or maybe because of it—I was given the gift of desperation. I eventually learned to be gentle with myself and to let others take charge when needed.

There is a gentleman I know that, for the first six months of his sobriety, would call his sponsor every morning because he felt so lost. His sponsor would tell him to brush his teeth, take a shower, get dressed, eat breakfast, and call him back. And when he did those things, his sponsor would tell him to go to work, go to a recovery meeting, and call him later. That man was a senior vice president at an investment company. Today, he has more than 30 years of sobriety—one day, one shower, one meeting at a time.

I had no idea how fragile I could be, but also how strong. I am a miracle, and I never take that lightly.

Lana E.

I remember waiting for my daughter and grandchildren outside the front doors of Sierra Tucson by the fountain. The sky seemed bluer than I had ever seen it, and the sound of the water and birds was much richer than I had remembered....

My logical mind told me it had probably been this way when they dropped me off 30 days before, but something miraculous had changed my perception. I was more aware. I was alive.

My daughter loaded my things in the back of her SUV as the two kids hugged and kissed me, squealing with joy. My daughter also hugged me, but with some restraint. I had betrayed her faith many times in the past so she was not all that eager to be hurt again. On our ride back to my house, Kelly, my daughter, asked what she could do to help me and was surprised at my answer. I asked her to go through my closet with me since that was my hiding place and to go to the store with me since that had been my main supplier. Change is hard, and here was where I needed to begin. After fulfilling both requests, she again asked what she could do, not realizing that for a person who could not ask for help in the past, this was huge. Next, I told Kelly that I had committed to going to a recovery meeting that evening and getting a sponsor. She reluctantly left knowing that it was now in my hands.

I had been going to Alcoholics Anonymous since 1983, so I knew where to go; this time, though, I was going to do it the way it was written. Surely, someone there would be willing to take me on. I was very nervous, yet excited, as I took my seat behind the woman who was giving out the coins for the meeting. Although I had attended this meeting previously, sometimes intoxicated, I had never seen her there before. When I announced I needed a 30-day sobriety chip and a "temporary" sponsor, she looked me in the eyes and said we would talk after the meeting.

I don't remember the meeting, just the fact that afterward she shared she had not been to this particular meeting since she had moved across town. But something that morning had told her she needed to be here. She said she fought the urge all day, then finally gave in and now she understood why. We made plans to attend a noon meeting the next day in another part of town. I wrote down the cross streets and we parted.

I went home and called my husband, who was back in our Kansas City, Missouri, home. He listened and wished me well with not much enthusiasm. Things between us were shaky at best.

The next morning I started my commitment for a better life, called my daughter to report the news of the prior evening, and got ready to really begin my recovery. I looked up the address of the noon meeting and drove to where I thought I was to meet Patricia. It was in the back of an auto repair garage. I was early so I went in and got a seat. Most of the people were homeless or close to it with lots of tattoos and missing teeth. I stuck out like a sore thumb. I hadn't felt this uncomfortable in a long time. The meeting started and all was right with the world. I heard stories that made me realize I hadn't gone as far down as I could have. When it was my turn, I shared my truth and fears and felt a part of something greater.

After the meeting, which Patricia had not attended, I spoke with a woman who appeared to have all her earthly belongings in a grocery cart. She suggested I might have gotten this meeting place confused with one a half-mile away. Oh my God, these coincidences seemed to be happening at every turn. I left a message with Patricia, which I'm sure sounded as though I was on the verge of hysteria. When we finally met, she explained to me the miracles that had happened in her life. She asked me to consider that maybe mine had been there all along—that maybe I had been too caught up in my disease and addiction to notice.

This began a healing process that continues today. I don't take the gifts that I received at Sierra Tucson for granted, and I still believe in miracles. I am one!

Paul N.

I left Sierra Tucson on my 27th birthday. The evening before my departure, my casita mates and I purposefully circled together, passed around my Sierra Tucson medallion, and they gently sang "Amazing Grace" to me. I hold that very medallion today, and after 24 years, find it comforting to recall the sounds of their voices....

The next morning, I woke up before dawn and sat silently in the community room, reflecting on the prior 30 days and fully acknowledging the life-changing significance of my Sierra Tucson experience. I felt ready to go but reluctant and anxious. I could barely imagine what it would be like to reenter my life in Atlanta. I looked out over the shadowy desert and resolved that the life that I left a mere one month prior felt enormously far way. I had grown so much, both emotionally and spiritually. I actually recognized and accepted myself in the story of my life; I was congruent.

At Sierra Tucson I explored trauma, addiction, and codependency. Physically I had quit smoking cigarettes, gave up alcohol and drugs, and gained a new clarity. I was rebirthed, faced my abuser, confronted my family of origin, and reassured my child within. Basically, I became an adult. In this way, I was a secure man, yet I felt shaky to leave the comfort and love of my newly found tribe.

In the van on the way to the airport, I was joined by the same two individuals who had shared the ride with me through the entry gates of Sierra Tucson. We acknowledged how significantly different the three of us looked. We hugged and waved goodbye. I was soon alone on the plane, and my reentry from orbit was solo. I'll admit that at the time, I compared my experience with that of an astronaut reentering from outer space: confident, prepared, exposed and vulnerable, all at the same time.

I can't remember how I got from the airport to my apartment—it was truly a fog—but I do remember reaching out to my Sierra Tucson buddies and spending that first evening at home on the phone. Together, we recalled every difficult and joyous detail of our Sierra Tucson experience, and supported each other in our transition back to Earth. I needed this connection more than anything.

On the second day home, I wasn't quite sure what to do with myself or my conflicting feelings. I remember setting up a small altar with my Sierra Tucson medallion, my Day by Day book, and a rock that I toted back from the desert in my luggage. I meditated and cried a bit with gratitude. I was still quite anxious and felt dreadfully exposed, but I was healing. With urgency, I arranged to join a reciprocal aftercare group at a local treatment center. This step, and the anticipated structure that it would provide, felt reassuring.

Later that day, I invited a friend over (the Sierra Tucson alum who encouraged me go to Sierra Tucson) for a healthy pasta dinner; I didn't want to be alone. What happened next might not seem like a monumental achievement to some, but it was for me. What happened was I slowly chopped vegetables for what seemed like hours. I chopped, and chopped, and chopped. I indulged in this Zen task, experienced it, and enjoyed it! This was new behavior. Something inside had certainly shifted. (Perhaps washing dishes would be next!)

So for the first 48 hours, I remember taking it easy, allowing myself time, establishing a structure, and reaching out to my tribe from Sierra Tucson. Still today, I'm involved with the Sierra Tucson Alumni community. We've all been through something special, something unique, and share a bond of support. Years later, I'm living a serene and grateful life with several advanced degrees, a loving and healthy family, a meaningful and purposeful career, and, most importantly, a solid recovery. It's been over 24 years since that first 48 hours at Sierra Tucson and, yes, like everyone else who has entered through those doors, I am a miracle. ▪

Chrisi H.

I went to Sierra Tucson for trauma and alcoholism 16 years after I had been gang raped in college. It was that horrific event that had put my drinking on a fast track. I stuffed all the feelings from the rape inside until I could no longer handle it....

It came to a head when, after having two daughters, ages 2 and 3 at the time, I realized that this was not what I wanted for myself. I didn't want to be an alcoholic mother. My girls didn't deserve that. While I had started at Alcoholics Anonymous a year prior, I couldn't go more than 30 days without relapsing. Then back-to-back DUIs convinced me it was time to make more of an effort. So I chose Sierra Tucson.

It was scary to think about leaving the security of Sierra Tucson when the time came. As I anticipated going home, I had mixed feelings. On one hand, I was so excited to see my girls but very aware that I was still so raw in the healing process. I knew all those feelings had to come up to come out, but I was comforted to think that it didn't have to happen all at once. Thinking back, I was just grateful that my girls were young enough at the time that they don't remember seeing a drunken mom. While they only know a sober mom, as adults themselves today, they also know my story.

The shame, along with the DUIs, prompted me to seek change. I was miserable, and I didn't want to be that type of mom or person. It wasn't the life I wanted to live. I was still carrying the shame of when I was raped. Although it shouldn't have had power over me, it did. Being raped and being a victim of that kind of violence during my first year in college was something that people didn't talk about then, so I stuffed it inside for a long time.

When I was dropped off at the airport following discharge, the realization of being back in the real world was bizarre. At Sierra Tucson, there was no TV or radio. There was very limited phone time with our families, and that was even awkward since we had to place calls at the nurses' station with them present. It was very different than it is now. There were no newspapers and no other contact with the outside world, so being dropped off at the airport was overwhelming. I had

had no caffeine or sugar while I was at Sierra Tucson, but I got a Diet Coke and M&M's at the airport. Everything about the airport was exciting and scary at the same time.

On my way home, I couldn't help but wonder what it was going to be like when I got home. I worried about a lot of things. I wondered if there were some bottles still around the house that I hadn't thrown away. I worried if the kids were going to be mad because I had been gone. And I was coming back to an alcoholic husband. Would he be drunk? At Family Week at Sierra Tucson, the first thing my husband said to me when he saw me was, "Are you fixed yet?" So it was scary coming home. There was an expectation that I would be "fixed" and that would be that. But I was not fixed. I felt raw and vulnerable. I felt younger than my kids, and yet, here I was with these little kids to raise.

It turned out my husband was happy to see me. I wasn't sure he was really happy to see me or if he was happy that he would once again have someone to take care of the kids since he wasn't a hands-on husband or dad. The kids were definitely happy to see me. I was back to being mom. I went to AA meetings and had my kids go with me. I had to get rides to and from because I didn't have a driver's license due to DUIs, but other than that, I jumped right back in to being a mom again. It made it hard that my husband was not supportive. In fact, later on, he decided that AA was a cult and that they stole me away and ruined our marriage.

Being back in my routine of going to meetings and being with my great sponsor who has helped me and loved me regardless of the times I relapsed were a great help in easing me back to reality. My sponsor, who is the same sponsor I have had all the years I have been in AA, has been a very important part of my reentry. I am very fortunate to have her.

However, the best gift I ever gave myself and my family was Sierra Tucson. It was also the hardest thing. I go to the Sierra Tucson Alumni Retreat every year. I have never missed a year. It recharges me each year for the upcoming holidays, too. Staying connected is a very important part of my recovery. Going to Sierra Tucson saved my life, and the tools I learned there continue to help me handle whatever life throws my way. We are all miracles.

Marcy D.

The only thing more daunting than passing by the behemoth sign at the entrance to Sierra Tucson that reads "Expect a Miracle" is passing by the sign at the exit that reads "You Are a Miracle." Both are huge benchmarks, equally weighted, and profoundly true....

What happened between the metaphoric signage was nothing less than a miracle for me, and I count it, to this day, as the single most significant event in my lifetime.

Like every other sojourner crossing over into recovery, my life had become unmanageable, and I found myself begging my Maker to answer my calls for help that I screamed out loud. I considered my arrival at Sierra Tucson as a beacon of hope, and the answer to my prayers. This is significant, as I resolved to take in every shred of wisdom from a brilliant cast of characters, both fellow residents and doctors, and anyone else who touched my life in the following 30 days. I began to write story after story about my experiences about life before treatment and my hopes for a future—any future. For the sake of real time, I am including a couple of the stories I wrote on my last day at Sierra Tucson, and in the first 48 hours thereafter.

BURNING EMBERS

The culmination of the Sierra Tucson experience crescendos in the beloved Kiva at dusk, just after the graduation ceremony. All the newly minted parolees proudly enter the circle clutching various pieces of papyrus on which they bared their souls over the past 30 days. The fire glowed brilliant orange, crackling and swirling in the building monsoon winds, sending translucent pieces of pain-drenched ash on paths of their own into the purgatory of the night sky.

The fire gained stature, as the winds grew stronger, as did the bravery and self-assurance of the tribe. Voices grew louder, and the anger of the past took the stage in a fiery breeze. Timelines were dashed into the funeral pyre, never to be retrieved. Letters to loved ones, bitter and accusatory began to char at the edges, then curl up and evaporate into thin air.

As the fire began to die down, with it the general shore-leave atmosphere, I left the Kiva with my timeline tucked under my arm. No burning tonight, there was too much good life written on those pages... bittersweet memories, and so many of them that had not come to mind for years.

My life has been nothing, if not rich. I have lived, loved, rejoiced, suffered and learned a great many things, and many of them the hard way. The pure and simple fact is that my life, in many ways, has only just begun. It is dawn at the edge of meaning, and I am up early...

THE FLIGHT PLAN

A wise and learned staff member named Mark, or "Mindful Mark," said to me at the end of my journey that by the time I got on the plane and activated my cell phone, which I did not miss by the way, the past month would seem like a dream. A mirage in the desert. I was leaving the "bubble" and safety of the nest where I was so well nurtured and cared for.

The avian metaphor holds a lot of meaning for me. The lesson is simple, yet ageless. Like the quails of Tucson, Ariz., whose coveys dwindled in numbers as the days passed, or the blue-footed Nazca boobies of the Galapagos, it truly is survival of the fittest. Harness the wisdom of the ages from those who have gone before you, protect yourself from danger, think before you act, and care for yourself and others. Before all else, be kind. Be kind to yourself, and to others. What a concept.

It is time to feather my own nest, wherever that may be, and thrive. "Go get a life," I have been told. I can do that. Failure to launch is no longer an option. It is a clear day. All systems go. Houston, I am ready for liftoff.

Life has not been perfect since the first 48 hours. I heeded the words of Mindful Mark and gathered my strength as I packed out of my comfort zone in the desert. The remarkable difference was that I had all the tools in my toolkit that I needed to succeed in my quest for continued sobriety and well-being.

Life became a balancing of the scales. I traded my marriage for an independent lifestyle that suits me well. My daughter has followed my example by becoming healthy, happy, and productive in her own right. The fear of failure was real, yet I did not let it reign. Other words of wisdom I learned at Sierra Tucson are that 98 percent of fear is unfounded. The odds were in my favor, and remain so. I built a safety net around myself with a brilliant team of professionals. I continue to see a naturopath and a therapist, and spend a considerable amount of time in various modes of self-care. So therein lies the truth: You really can go home again, and survive, and thrive. I do believe in miracles. I am one.

Tim M.

I remember my last day at Sierra Tucson like it was yesterday. It was a day full of anxiety and excitement. The anxiety began well before leaving. Could I actually do this thing called recovery? I didn't want to lose the hopefulness I'd begun to feel. Would leaving this healing cocoon be a smart thing?...

I kept hearing stories of others relapsing immediately after treatment. All I could focus on was what the therapists continued to share, "It's good to have a healthy fear."

I drove 1,300 miles to get to Sierra Tucson. I had never been to treatment and I drove because I had wanted the ability to leave. It was my way of having a sense of control. I requested that the nurse who admitted me would also discharge me. I was grateful this request had worked out. The nurse walked me out to the vehicle, gave me a hug and handed me a silver guardian angel—a small token, yet it meant so much to me that I carried it everywhere.

When pulling out of the parking lot, I saw the sign "You Are a Miracle." I was amazed at how 30 days had changed my perspective. When I arrived the sign read "Expect a Miracle." Then I thought, "Yeah, right." Today, I was in agreement: I am a miracle.

My roommate while in treatment lived locally and offered me a place to stay for the night before hitting the road home. That ended up not being a good decision on my part; I'm pretty sure he had already relapsed. I was grateful for the bed, but I was up and out of there early the next day.

One thing I was very aware of was that I needed consistency to remain on the path of recovery. It was not wise of me to go out on a limb and take chances. I did my best to emulate my daily routine around the schedule I had maintained in treatment. I was committed to 90 meetings in 90 days, so before I started my journey home, I attended a 12-Step meeting. As I began my journey home, my mind became overwhelmed with emotions—everything from loneliness to the fear of the unknown. I started repeating the Serenity Prayer over and over, and in time, those feelings passed.

Halfway home, I checked in to a hotel. The next morning with meal plan in hand, I walked into a restaurant. I immediately sized the place up. Meaning, I noticed there was no place for me to sit. One addiction I worked on in treatment was binge eating disorder. I was a large man, and the restaurant only had booths. I began to go into a shame spiral. I was able to pause the negative thoughts by asking myself the question, "What can I do in this moment to take care of myself?" I ended up placing my order to go and eating it on the tailgate of my pickup. I had a self-care boundary that I would no longer eat in my vehicle, and I wasn't about to break that boundary one day out of treatment. I remember sitting there in the morning sun with tears of joy streaming down my face. "So this is what self-care feels like," I thought.

It was late when I finally arrived home. I walked into my apartment to find that while I was gone, my sink had overflowed. The smell was horrible. Here I was at another decision point. I wanted to punch the wall in anger. Again the quiet voice of reason arrived, "What can I do in this moment to take care of myself?" I went into the bedroom, closed the door, opened the window for fresh air and ended the day sober, abstinent, and full of gratitude. I am a miracle!

Janet S.

Six hours from departing Sierra Tucson for home and I was tired, fearful, happy, lonely, hopeful, sad, and, hopefully, willing. As I anticipated leaving Sierra Tucson after my 30-day stay, I felt a surge of adrenaline fueled by fear, yet an undeniable excitement to see my kids, and then again, fear. Fear of leaving the "bubble."....

Must I leave this safety, this beauty, and these people? People I have come to know and love at a much deeper level than I have known most people in my life prior to this immersion. Will they be OK? Will I be OK?

They talk about the tools I have been given here. What are they? I was afraid to ask for fear of appearing stupid. What have I gained here? I didn't fully know, yet I felt different. Did I have what I needed to survive sober, let alone happy, joyous, and free? I felt really scared that I wouldn't be able to do this outside the safety of Sierra Tucson. I was also fearful of my husband. I had to stay sober because I was certain there were no extra chances left with him. A well-known attorney, a powerful political figure, an imposing and controlling person in my life, I could see my husband having no hesitation to take our kids (8 and 10 at the time) away from me and drop me on the street with nothing if I drank again after this investment. No one would blame him. My family would be let down and very angry if that were to happen. I loved my kids too much to ever lose the opportunity to be in their lives. I was very uncertain about my marriage, but losing everything because of drinking was not going to be the way I was going to let things transpire.

While at Sierra Tucson, I avoided working on my marriage as much as I could have and should have. I was guilty of omission, leaving out facts. Should I have mentioned that we were going on a private ship to the Bahamas in a month? No, they might have said I couldn't go. Should I have spent time working on my marriage? The risk was that that might have increased my length of stay.

These were the challenges I faced in the first 48 hours. I hoped I didn't set myself up for failure. I asked my husband to throw out the Xanax the week prior. I never acknowledged it was there to anyone. My doctor prescribed it so I wouldn't need wine. Xanax had never been a problem since I didn't like taking medications. It did, however, take courage to ask my husband to throw it out before I came home. I had wanted a safety net in case I couldn't cope with my feelings. I guess that during the last week in treatment at Sierra Tucson, my fear of finding a new addiction won over my fear of not making it through my feelings and life. I was very fearful—fearful of life, fearful of being. I was so glad we worked on my fear while I was at Sierra Tucson, as well as being present, awake, and aware. I hoped those lessons could be carried home.

I remember thinking how much I would miss this place, the sounds of coyotes and the mountain vistas. The ever-amazing Santa Catalina Mountains. I came to believe while walking on the trail that they could handle my problems. I imagined the pioneers crossing them and the problems they must have left behind. The challenges they must have faced. I grew to love those mountains, ever stoic, filled with beauty, always changing. A cloud covers them for a minute and the top is covered with snow, and moments later, the sun is laying its beautiful rays across the valleys in ever-changing patterns of light and shades of green. They became my Higher Power and I would miss them so much. They showed me a path to spiritual peace. Would that exist at home?

I left so happy to have 30 days alcohol-free. I had never been able to achieve 30 hours without wine, let alone 30 days. In anticipation of going to Sierra Tucson, my goal was to achieve 30 days of no wine. Even though I didn't know what to expect, my experience at Sierra Tucson turned out to be so much more than I anticipated. I surrendered, I guess. Surrendered to something I didn't know or understand on a drunken plane ride to a place I had never been, to spend 30 days with people I did not know. The most impactful thing I heard when I arrived was from the medical director. He said,

"A paradox: Sometimes the thing you think is the worst thing in your life becomes the best."

In the morning when I was to leave, everything was packed, and I enjoyed breakfast with all of the people I had grown to love. It was "Clap Out and Tears"—a tradition that signified someone was leaving, an acknowledgment of moving on. Knowing it was my last breakfast, I felt so much love and compassion from my heart, a place I had not been able to truly access for a long time. We were all broken, like the toys on the Island of Misfit Toys from the movie Rudolph the Red-Nosed Reindeer.

I didn't want to leave, yet I had to get home. I missed my kids so much. What about my marriage? What about my husband's drinking? Will I make it without drinking at the airport or on the plane? Tears and more tears. I was going to miss the beautiful view in the dining hall, the caring and loving therapists, and the staff that exposed me to many thought processes I never knew existed: Eastern Thought; Recovery Thought; Native American Thought; finding peace from within. The peace I found at Sierra Tucson gave me a light inside I never had before. I was going to miss the air—calmer, lighter, softer, lacking tension. The Santa Catalina Mountains will forever be my Higher Power.

The van arrived to go to the airport. It came time for me to leave the bubble of safety surrounded by the most beautiful mountains I have ever seen—mountains big enough to take my problems and fears and majestically hold them as they had for so many before me, healing parts of me that had been in so much pain and making me human again, vulnerable, loving, and humble. As we departed, I reflected back on my journey, which was barely memorable since my blood alcohol content was around 0.3. It was so strange to leave feeling full of such gratitude, with tears of joy streaming inside my heart and welling up in my eyes. The colors and beauty of the surrounding nature were bursting in my head. What a sad person I was when I arrived. "You are a miracle," I wanted to shout to everyone who works at Sierra Tucson and to Sierra Tucson itself: "You are a miracle."

Traffic. Noise. Looking out the back window, I remember staring at the beauty to capture every last glimpse and forever burn a picture of the grandeur in my brain. More traffic and noise—sounds I haven't heard in 30 days, people rushing to work or wherever they are going. I remember how strange it felt as I reentered society. I had been gone from the craziness. One of the therapists had said, "What an amazing world it would be if everyone took 30 days off to work on themselves." It was a strange feeling to be back in the real world. People driving, caught up in their lives, with no chance to experience the cleansing I had been through.

At the airport, the first things on my list were a Diet Pepsi and a cigarette. Or should I not indulge in that soda? Thirty days of no caffeine, sugar, or soda. To blow it or not to blow it? It didn't take much processing to decide to go for it. To me, giving in to a Diet Pepsi craving that was much stronger than my wine craving was worth it. My mind was worried about access to alcohol. I didn't want to be one of those people who drank at the airport as soon as they got out of treatment. I played the thought of drinking in my head and imagined the horror on the face of my kids and husband picking up a drunken mom. Kids who so desperately wanted me home and didn't fully understand why I was gone. Kids I missed every day. The Diet Pepsi won.

My mind replayed the trip to Tucson on the way back through the airport. I was so filled with gratitude by how wonderful I felt physically, spiritually, and emotionally. I thought about how I only had to make it onto the plane, and then past the drink service, and then I would be home. I felt so good. The drink cart was right near the entrance door on the plane; it called my name for a minute and I congratulated myself for not staring at it too much. I found my seat and hoped whoever was sitting around me chose not to drink. It wasn't a burning desire to drink. It was an uncertainty and lack of self-trust.

The arrival home was wonderful. I felt so much joy from the warm welcome I received and the excitement of the kids. My husband was very welcoming as well. The car ride home was great. There was so much to catch up on.

Yet once at the house, I felt less steady. What was expected of me? How will what I learned in Arizona be carried over to Ohio? The joy and attention from my kids carried me far. I thought it through and realized two things: I needed to get to a recovery meeting within 24 hours of arriving home, and if I tried to keep my schedule as similar as I could to my routine in Arizona, I may have a better chance. After an exciting dinner of catching up, I headed upstairs to read to the kids. I brought everything upstairs so I did not have to return downstairs. The kitchen, family room, and just downstairs in general had way too many triggers associated with drinking.

Reading recovery literature in bed and asleep by 10 p.m. had become my norm at Sierra Tucson, so that was what I did. I was reading Drinking: A Love Story by Caroline Knapp. Biographies by people who were in recovery became my new obsession. This book in particular really struck a chord with me. I could relate so much to the author's story.

The next day I was up at 6:30 a.m. to get the kids ready for school. It was so enjoyable to wake up clear-headed after a good night's sleep. No hangover while preparing lunches, no guilt for my behavior the night before. This new freedom was a big one for me to process. After dropping the kids off at school and driving to work out, I realized I had nothing to feel bad about. I didn't do anything wrong. Gone, at least for today, was the hungover, guilt-filled morning of mentally beating myself up over my drinking and what I may have said or done to my husband or a friend on a drunk dial. I began the process of releasing the guilt and shame mentally and physically. I literally felt a weight being lifted, as if a heavy winter coat was being discarded on a warm, early spring day.

Working out was so much better without a hangover. Talking to people was so much more fulfilling when I didn't feel a need to hide who I was or what I was doing when no one was watching. There was no longer two of me fighting against each other—the image I tried to present to the world versus the dark side of who I really was. I was becoming one whole human being, and with that, I was definitely living in joy. Many might call it a pink cloud, yet I can say today, eleven and a half years later, that joy is deeper and still a daily part of my life. During these years I have had dark moments and challenging situations, yet never the darkness I felt prior to Sierra Tucson. There is always light in my life. I strive for authenticity.

Again, following my pattern of trying to live as closely to the Sierra Tucson lifestyle as I could, I started journaling daily and reading meditation books every morning and night. I would challenge myself throughout my day to become present at a stoplight or in a meeting. I had learned at Sierra Tucson how quickly I could mentally exit life. My thought process became mind, body, and spirit. When I am troubled, I focus on which of those three it is, and how can I change it.

I went to my first Alcoholics Anonymous meeting at 1 p.m. the day after I returned home. This was my home group and I adored many people there prior to Sierra Tucson. When I arrived and saw my sponsor, she commented on how good

I looked during various times throughout the meeting. She observed something had really changed in me, yet she couldn't name it. She said she had not seen as big of a transformation so quickly in anyone as she had seen in me. I appeared calm, confident, and more comfortable in my own skin, happy and serene. I was eager, willing, and ready to get involved. I truly felt most comfortable and safe at AA meetings. I felt fortunate that I had a sponsor and base of people I knew in AA before I went to treatment. Now having returned from Arizona, I really began to feel a part of AA rather than a drunk hiding in shame in the corner. I was very, very grateful for my experience at Sierra Tucson. The wisdom and experience I had gained there was more than many who were trying to recover would ever be able to experience. It moved me ahead in my recovery by leaps and bounds.

After the meeting, I decided to swim laps. Swimming had always been a big part of my life. In recovery, I found swimming to be a great opportunity to relieve stress and bring me to the present. The first 10 to 15 laps were spent processing thoughts, my mind going fast; after those initial laps I was awake, aware, and present. It would help me work through depression, stress, anger, and really any emotion that became bigger than me. It centered me and allowed me to be calm. I think the breathing-in swimming really helped, as well as the immersion into water. It made it a lot harder not to be present.

Relaxed, calm, and excited, it was now time to pick up the kids. The teachers at pick-up were complimentary on my appearance. A couple of the teachers knew where I had been and gave me the knowing smile and eye contact. I shared with my children's primary teachers where I was going prior to leaving so they would be aware and notice if there were any changes in the kids. They were understanding, respectful, and supportive. The kids also came for Family Week at Sierra

Tucson, so they were out of school for a week. My happiness in being back and seeing the kids after school was amazing.

I felt confident and pretty for the first time in a long time. Many people complimented me on my appearance, noting that something had changed that they could not identify. I had been taking care of myself. I decided only to share information about where I had been when I found it safe to do so. I admit I was a bit fearful at first of entering AA meetings and the "wrong" person seeing me. I quickly learned anyone who was there came for the same reason I did. I also came to understand that most people were not as obsessed with where I was and what I was doing as I thought.

Unfortunately, I do not believe my husband set a boundary on what he told others about where I was. It made for some uncomfortable times wondering what people thought and some conversations or comments I wasn't sure how to interpret. I was grateful for the line "what other people think of me is none of my business" that I had learned at Sierra Tucson.

The second evening home was much like the first: homework, dinner, and time with the kids. They were so forgiving and so in the moment. They were my first joy in recovery, as they accepted the fact that I had changed. On the second evening, I choose to go to a meeting. At the beginning, my family did not understand my need for meetings when they were home. "Why didn't I go while they were in school?" they wondered. I just had to go. I learned that even though they may not understand, I had to be selfish about my recovery. I had often heard the phrase, "Anything you put before your recovery, you will lose."

By the time I returned from Sierra Tucson, I had a true understanding of my rock bottom and that if the people around me weren't there to hold me up financially and emotionally, I would have been homeless and living on the streets. The fact that I lived in suburbia, drove a nice car, and had a picture-perfect life from the outside had nothing to do with my efforts. My efforts were focused on two things before I left for Arizona: living a lie and trying to make my exterior appear as if everything was OK, then drinking wine around 5 p.m. until I blacked out every night. That was my life and I did it every day for years.

Upon my return home, I also focused on following everything that was laid out in my continuing care plan. For over three years, I remained in counseling with the therapist who was recommended to me by Sierra Tucson. I went every week when I first returned and throughout my first year, as well as through difficult times later in my recovery. Unfortunately, my husband was not amenable to marriage counseling and Al-Anon, as was suggested to him. I did not let that deter me from pursuing my recovery, though. His decision fortified my resolve in making my recovery my own.

Looking back at those first couple of days is rewarding. They were hard—hard enough that I don't want to do it again—yet they were filled with joy and tremendous learning. I realized I had been given a gift that not everyone is as fortunate to receive. The experiences in those 30 days served as a springboard into a new way of living, including exposure to ways of thinking and spirituality I would have never been exposed to in more traditional settings. From Day One at home to today, I have used my experience, spirituality, and joy for life that I gained in the foothills of the Santa Catalina Mountains to benefit my recovery and help others. I have returned to Sierra Tucson with tears of joy in my eyes. The minute I see those mountains from the plane, I am forever grateful for this new way of living.

I return to Sierra Tucson as often as possible for the Alumni Retreat every fall, and have returned to speak to residents and share my story. It is a gift I give myself to renew my recovery and stay close to the place that has allowed me to live the life I live today. I simply cannot summarize the gratitude I feel. My wish is that you find this gift, as well.

Eric S.

When the time came to leave Sierra Tucson, I did not know what to expect back at home. While it was a big decision to be in a therapeutic setting for four weeks, I knew going home would also be a return to daily reality. I was nervous about the support network I needed to implement....

I had an immediate mission, and that was to avoid drinking in the airport or on the plane ride home. Drinking and isolating myself went hand in hand, so I knew it was going to be a challenge. I still had the stone given to me during graduation at Sierra Tucson, with the word "miracle" on it, so I held that in my hand. I also kept a full water bottle handy, and tried to stay mindful—one journey completed turns into another journey to complete.

Getting readjusted to home made me really process everything I had learned. Based on all the great people at Sierra Tucson—amazing therapists and fellow "lodge warriors"—I felt I had some positive energy and experience moving me in the right direction. I wanted to keep this momentum going by being intentional, fully aware of my surroundings and emotions.

Waking up early had been a challenge prior to Sierra Tucson, so I made this part of my morning routine. By waking up at the same time and meditating, I tried to maintain some of the regular experience that had helped me in treatment at Sierra Tucson. I also wrote down my feelings and mood in a journal each morning. I found it more valuable to check in with myself regularly than to give in to the urge to make all the adjustments right away.

I followed the continuing care advice given to me by Sierra Tucson staff and went to an intensive outpatient program each day, and circled back to the doctor who had recommended Sierra Tucson. She paired me up with a new psychiatrist who was familiar with addiction recovery. That was one of the things I made a personal priority.

The bottom line is, I trivialized alcohol and its impact. The decision to cut out alcohol came down to self-respect. I left Sierra Tucson and wanted to hold on to that clarity, that positive momentum, that sense of gratitude that the rest of my life could be reset on a healthier plane. Life doesn't give us a whole lot of chances to select a better path. Recovery has given me yet another chance to look forward to a life fully lived. ▨

Maureen K.

My journey to Sierra Tucson consisted of drinking most of my adult life, the loss of two executive positions, and, ultimately, a DUI. My last employer gave me the gift of recovery by supporting treatment in an alcoholic treatment program. I was more than ready to find out the "whys" of my destructive behavior. I was at the end and needed help....

I was 15 days sober when I went to Sierra Tucson and embraced the warmth and love. I was ready to do the work and discover who I am.

Upon starting my journey at Sierra Tucson, I did not know what life held for me or what it would look like at the end. I had no job, my husband was done with me, and I was not sure if there would be an "us" for us any longer. All I knew was that I had to figure out what brought me to the place where I was, and I had to want recovery for myself this time—not to save my marriage, a job, or for any other reason. I needed to want it for Maureen!

My husband picked me up at Sierra Tucson after my 34-day stay. He had attended Family Week and visited on Sundays, but now it was just going to be us. We do not have any children together, and his children are grown, so we live alone. My husband is a beer drinker. I had to be honest with myself on what that meant to me. I was open and honest throughout my treatment and knew I needed a plan upon leaving, and I was scared to leave. I felt safe and supported at Sierra Tucson. I committed to doing 90 meetings in 90 days upon leaving and getting a sponsor. My insurance did not extend to an intensive outpatient program, so I knew it was up to me.

Saying goodbye to Sierra Tucson and my new family was harder than I could have imagined. Upon leaving, I saw the "You Are a Miracle" sign and I cried. I was sad to leave but forever grateful I was taking the love of Sierra Tucson with me, as well as an invaluable toolbox for living.

I so clearly remember that first night arriving home—everything felt different. I was different. I had traveled much throughout my career but had never been away from home or my husband for more than two weeks in 12 years of marriage. It was as if everything was a new discovery. I walked around looking at my beautiful home and wanted to open the windows for fresh air, to be able to breathe. My husband was kind and thoughtful. We had stopped for dinner, so it was already late. I was tired, emotions running high, and I just wanted to say my prayers and go to sleep. My husband held me that first night and told me he was glad I was home. It was a good start.

My first morning back to home following treatment, I called my family members after breakfast and told them I was home. The voice messages and emails received while I was away were overwhelming, as I had not told anyone outside of the family that I would be gone. I put them aside, prayed, and got ready for an Alcoholics Anonymous meeting.

I had tried to stop drinking many times before Sierra Tucson and had been to AA. I had had a sponsor but never got past the Fourth Step. I knew this time was going to be different—it had to be different. I had truly surrendered, and Sierra Tucson had taught me that the gift of recovery was for life. I had my tools and was ready to jump in. I had received my 30-day sobriety chip at Sierra Tucson but identified myself at the AA meeting as a newcomer. I didn't recognize many people, but they remembered me. I shared that I had just gotten out of treatment and I wanted what they had. I committed to finding a sponsor in the first week of being home and working the Steps. I knew I had to work all of the Steps this time and in order—no skipping to forgiveness.

The meeting, one of which I still attend today, brought me comfort and a sense of familiarity. I was home! I took my newcomer packet with all the phone numbers. The support was incredible.

My license was to be suspended within days because of the DUI; my husband let me know he was going out of town for a few days and asked if I would be OK home alone. It was truly the first moment I realized it was all up to me. Nothing could make me drink, and no one was going to keep me sober but myself. I was not good at asking for help, but I wanted recovery more than anything. I would (and did) call the numbers I received for support and for rides to meetings. I wrote in my journal and prayed often for strength and in gratitude.

Sierra Tucson taught me to be present, to be mindful, to stay in the moment, and to be accountable. Recovery had to come first. My marriage was not going to heal overnight, my husband was not going to change and stop drinking, and the consequences (DUI and unemployment) of my past behaviors needed to be faced with grace and dignity. To have or do any of this, I needed God and my toolbox, and take one day at a time. I will be forever grateful for both and Sierra Tucson for helping me see the miracles in life and believing I am one, too.

Reflecting back on my first 48 hours after Sierra Tucson, and now several years of recovery, the Promises have come true and miracles continue. I am not perfect; life is not perfect. It is only possible by the grace of God, my Higher Power, taking one day at a time, using my toolbox, having the ability to forgive myself, and never giving up. The gift of recovery is for life, and so is my foundation and friends from Sierra Tucson! When times are tough or seem impossible, I remember to reach out to others and pick up my toolbox. I am Sierra Tucson "safe." I am a miracle.

Sally S.

Leaving Sierra Tucson formally started when the driver arrived to take me to the airport. I thought, "I can leave Sierra Tucson and get on with my life!"

I was at Sierra Tucson for the Mood & Anxiety Program— not alcohol, or drugs, or sex addiction, or chronic pain, or an eating disorder. It was for mood—plain and simple....

My mood was the issue and it was killing me. I was at the lowest possible point when I checked myself in. And checking out, I was ready to conquer my world.

While I was in treatment, I attended every class. I read the books. I did the assignments. And I did my timeline. I walked the track. I stayed away from TV and the internet. I made few phone calls. In the process, I found my strong inner self. Now, I just had to take her out into the real world and survive.

The airport was the first time I felt totally free from everyone and everything at Sierra Tucson. No longer "Depressed Sally," I was so excited to drink a Pepsi and eat a fast-food hamburger, but ugh, they sure upset my tummy. (Nobody told me that they retrain your stomach while you are at Sierra Tucson. Sugar and fatty foods are no longer your friends.)

Getting off the plane and seeing my husband and puppy, Sadie, brought the biggest smile to my face. Their hugs were so comforting and I was home, home, home. Going to bed that night, I thanked God for so much and promised I wouldn't let Him down.

Day One, Sadie and I had the house to ourselves. I went through my normal routine of making the bed, picking up the house and sitting on the back patio to drink my coffee and snuggle with Sadie. Bam! I start thinking negative thoughts; I had gone away to change, but nothing at home had changed. The fear of failure and depression was starting in on me so fast. Help! I hadn't been home even 48 hours. Tools, tools, tools—I struggled to recall—what had I learned? Argh! I told myself to think, think, think. What were the changes that I had planned to make? I needed to remember those changes.

OK, breathe. I assured myself: I can do this. Yes I can!

I then emailed my cousin about the real estate school she attended and she sent me the phone number. "Relax, it is just a call," I told myself. "You can't fail; you are already at the bottom. Call, call, call!" OK, call made. When? Shit! Classes start in two days! Am I really ready for this? Can I do this? I am a strong, independent woman. I conquered the challenge course at Sierra Tucson. I climbed that damn pole and crossed those damn lily pads. This was nothing compared to that. Take a breath, go for a walk, and do it!

Two days later I walked into the classroom and looked for someone safe to sit beside. I confidently introduced myself: "Hi, my name is Sally. What is yours?"

Eight months later, Casey and I are BFFs, and working for the same real estate company. We are kicking butt, and I continue to encourage others and myself with the tools I received from Sierra Tucson. I never forget my Sierra Tucson toolbox. I take it with me daily. ▧

Amy L.

There are many things in my life I don't remember; for example, what I had for lunch yesterday, or, even more accurately, the food binges I went on while I was blacked out. Or how I made it home safely way too many nights....

Nonetheless, there are some things that are so burned into my memory that I am convinced that even when I am old and senile, I will remember the final days of Sierra Tucson and the few days that followed.

I found myself in Tucson after years of binge eating, binge drinking, and trying to self-medicate my mood swings and substance-induced mania with over-the-counter sleeping pills. To say it plainly, I was a hot mess. And finally, I was done. I was willing to do whatever it took not to feel this way anymore. I wanted more from my life then what I had, and praise God, I had people around me who knew the right place to help me start that journey.

After a 45-day stay at Sierra Tucson, I was set to discharge on a Saturday afternoon. I had learned a lot in those 45 days, and the most important and upsetting thing I learned was that I was not to be trusted. I didn't even trust myself. Knowing that I hated flying, and recovering from a pretty significant anxiety disorder and a slew of other mental health diagnoses, I had the courage to ask my aunt to pick me up from Sierra Tucson and bring me home to Cincinnati. She happily obliged, and on a beautiful Saturday afternoon, my loving aunt and uncle picked me up with the one thing I had been craving for 45 days (relax, it was only a Diet Coke). Man, that was the best Diet Coke I had ever had in my whole life! Seriously.

We drove back to Phoenix in a comfy rental car; I sat in the back seat and marveled at the beautiful scenery I had failed to absorb on the drive down just six weeks prior. My aunt and uncle chatted with me, keeping conversation light while also kindly laying down some appropriate ground rules. I was returning to Cincinnati and staying at their home until I was able to get back on my feet. It had been a long time since I lived in someone else's home (10 years, going to college). I appreciated the ground rules; I had learned to appreciate and depend on boundaries.

When we arrived in Phoenix, I was faced with the decision of what we should have for dinner. Having been in eating disorder treatment for the past six weeks, I believed that the way I responded would be carefully considered. I was so afraid to say anything, but I said, "I have no idea what to say. I've not had to make choices about my food in six weeks. Do you have any suggestions?" We landed at a restaurant that had a wonderful menu with everything from sushi to steak. Perfect!

At Sierra Tucson, I was strongly encouraged to attend one of the West Coast aftercare programs when my residential care ended. My parents (who lived several hours away from me and were informed by phone that I was checking myself into treatment) and I decided that I didn't need it. We all felt that I was going back home to a loving, healthy environment and that I would be able to find a network of outpatient support to bridge the care from Sierra Tucson to the real world.

Sadly, as it turned out, those resources were not readily available in my area of the country at that time. And while I did return to a very loving and healthy environment, I sometimes regret not taking that wise advice from the Sierra Tucson professionals and experts. Residential aftercare isn't for everyone, but hindsight being 20/20, I do wish I would have heeded their advice. Now, eating disorder recovery centers are more readily available in my hometown; if I were transitioning today, perhaps the available intensive outpatient programs would be just what I needed. But they weren't available, and I am willing to say that my recovery suffered from the choices I made with my parents.

Now, back to the sushi: it was delicious! It was my first time in six weeks eating a meal with people who were not on staff at Sierra Tucson. Although I was not actually being watched by my family members and every single patron and employee in the restaurant, I sure felt like it. Being out in public at a restaurant was overwhelming. For the last six weeks, I was told when to get up, when to go to bed, what to eat, and where to be and when. And at that time when my whole world had crumbled around me, it was exactly what I needed. Clearly, my best decision-making landed me in a rehab facility for 45 days, so maybe it was someone else's turn to make decisions on my behalf.

We went back to the hotel, and I followed the suggestions my therapist had given me for my transition: remove the bathroom scale and make sure the mini bar is clear of alcohol and sweets, etc. I did all of that. My aunt and I inspected the hotel room and removed any items that would tempt me to stumble from my fresh, new recovery.

I got ready for bed. Then the second greatest thing happened. I got to listen to my iPod! At that time, I didn't have an iPhone, and Sierra Tucson did not allow residents to have iPods on campus. So, this was my first chance to plug in some headphones and fill my ears with the sweet sounds of Adam Levine and all the other music I had missed for so long. (Eye-roll all you want; Adam Levine is my happy place!)

I lay down on the hotel bed, which, I mentally noted, was not much different from my Sierra Tucson bed, and actively planned out what the next day was going to look like. I hate flying, and to prepare for sitting by myself on the plane, I followed the plan my therapist and I made before leaving the Sierra Tucson "bubble." I created a playlist that would more than cover the flights home—it was music that would distract, calm, and help me relax as I travel home. I visualized what I was going to wear on the plane, what I was going to eat for breakfast, what I wasn't going to eat on the plane, and how I was going to be sure to let my aunt and uncle know how grateful

I was for them to accompany me home. I finally fell asleep, for the first time in a long time outside the walls of Sierra Tucson. I slept an entire night without having nightmares, sweating, vomiting, or taking pills. It was then that I began to believe that I could do this. I could stay sober. I could stay clean. And I could make healthy decisions for myself.

The next morning, we got up. I wore the clothes I had envisioned the previous night. I ate the breakfast I had planned, and we went to the airport. As we got closer to the airport, I could feel my body tense up, my head got a little foggy, and I started to sweat. I remember closing my eyes, going to my safe place, and saying over and over to myself, "Just breathe. It's not that hard. Just breathe. It's OK, you're safe. Just breathe." I said it over and over and over. And then, I opened my eyes and I was safe; I was OK and the anxiety was gone. I thought to myself, "Wow! That stuff really works! OK, let's do this."

We got on the plane, I found my seat, pulled out my neck pillow, put my earbuds in my ears, closed my eyes, and breathed. In and out, all the way down to my belly. Over and over and over. In and out. I was safe. No one was going to hurt me. The plane was safe and I was going to be just fine. I kept telling myself that and pictured sitting in my safe place.

Next thing I knew, my shoulder was bumped by the drink and snack cart. I opened my eyes and I was met with the kind smile of the flight attendant. She offered me a drink, a snack, or a soda. Before I could even think, words flew out of my mouth. "No, thanks. I'm good." I literally shocked myself, mainly because I didn't even register what she was asking. I had already decided that I wasn't going to have anything, not even water. I just knew, that for me, that was the safest thing to do.

We landed back home in Cincinnati. It was mid-November, and I realized that I had missed fall! The leaves had turned, most had already fallen, and Earth was preparing for winter. I was so disappointed that I had missed it; fall in the Midwest is my favorite time of year. However, when I thought about it, just like the change of season—leaves turning, dying and falling away—I was doing the same thing in a way. I had spent time letting go of dead things in my life, things that caused me to be physically, mentally, and emotionally ill. I changed my own colors, my own opinions, my own behaviors, and dropped the things from my life that were dead. I dropped a job that did not support my sobriety; I cut ties with "friends" who didn't understand I had a problem; and I changed relationships with family members so that I wouldn't continue to live in a cycle of codependence and shame.

I was home now. I was in a safe place with people who loved me and wanted nothing more than for me to do well. They also knew it was a process and graced me with time, space to breathe, and ears with which to listen.

I am writing this now, eight years later, almost to the day that I entered Sierra Tucson. I look back on this journey I have been on, and it's amazing to see the blessings I have received. It hasn't been perfect. I have learned a lot, and I have stayed sober. My meal plan still challenges me, but I continue to work on my recovery. I went to Sierra Tucson thinking I may have an eating disorder (insert eye-roll here) and left acknowledging that I am also an alcoholic, codependent, anxiety-ridden, depressed individual with a history of trauma. That's a lot to carry; however, I am empowered knowing that there is a solution. And it's the knowledge that I am a miracle that helps me stay focused on the solution, no matter how many times I veer off course. ▨

Tom N.

I don't remember much about arriving at Sierra Tucson. I was pretty out of it. I do remember waking up in Desert Flower stabilization unit after 16 hours of much-needed sleep, thinking, "Twenty-nine more days in this place? How the hell am I gonna make it?" I was excited and scared....

Shortly after that, I was released into the community and assigned a room. The first few days were spent getting acclimated. There were doctor appointments, therapy meetings, group therapy meetings, lodge meetings, morning check-ins and evening check-ins. I was given a daily schedule, which was incredibly refreshing. I was told when to get up, when the lights were going off and where I needed to be every minute of the day. Never having had structure in my life, I welcomed it gratefully.

Foraging for food three times a day was a new experience, but once I mastered it, I realized the food was pretty good—there was pudding! At the end of the first week I was still thinking, "Twenty-three more days in this place? How the hell am I gonna make it?"

When it got down to one week left to go, I remember thinking, "I have to leave in seven days? How am I gonna handle that?" I found myself excited and scared, again.

With a suitcase full of books and a notepad full of phone numbers of friends whom I just knew would be friends for life, I hugged everyone one last time, jumped in the van, and headed for the airport. It felt eerily similar to the time, at 19 years old, when I loaded up my car and left Wisconsin for California, heading off alone into the unknown. Only now I was 54 years old and I was returning to a life—my life—parts of which would never be the same again.

I was fortunate to still have my business to return to, and, after 30 days away, it desperately needed my attention. I hadn't lost my home and was so grateful to have had someone tending my two dogs. Would they even remember me? It felt like a lifetime since I'd seen them last.

I'd heard stories of people relapsing at the airport. Not having been a big drinker, I wasn't so worried about that. Airport bars weren't serving my drug of choice. As I found my seat on the mostly empty plane to Los Angeles, a flight attendant struck up a conversation. "Heading home?" she asked.

"Yep!" I replied with a huge smile on my face. "Can't wait to get back."

"Were you in Arizona for business or pleasure?" she asked. Ahh. The first dilemma.

My family always worked hard to hide any form of "untidiness." We stuffed feelings deep down inside, never addressed them, and never, never, never shared them with complete strangers. Feelings of shame and guilt were all I knew—until Sierra Tucson. I had new tools now and new ways of dealing with my feelings, not to mention dealing with my family. Boundaries! Oh my God - BOUNDARIES! One of the biggest gifts from Sierra Tucson was a crystal-clear understanding of boundaries.

"I was in rehab for a month!" I told the flight attendant proudly. OK, I had boundaries down pat but I was still working on possible issues with oversharing!

The plane touched down, I turned on my phone, which dinged repeatedly, announcing messages and texts. Two high-profile clients wanted to meet with me the following day. I observed the feeling of overwhelm that had been so swift in taking me down prior to my exodus to Sierra Tucson. The key word there is observed. I recognized the feeling, but refused to get caught up in it. That was new!

I ordered an Uber from the airport and talked about rehab with my driver the entire trip home. Oversharing again, I know, but he seemed generally interested. I walked into the house wondering how the dogs would react. My boy, Tony, cocked his head and gave me a look of "WTF?" I watched as he realized who I was and came bounding over, nearly knocking me down. Lola, my girl, knew immediately who I was and she clearly remembered how upside down life had been. She sat back and looked at me dubiously, not sure she could trust me again. It was painful to experience but on a deeper level, I understood. She was a sensitive being, and I had to work to regain her trust.

I went for my phone and realized I had left it in the Uber car. SHIT! I sent the driver a note from my computer and he responded, "I'm in a parking lot near the airport. You know, where all the Uber drivers wait!" No. I didn't know. I had no freaking idea. A slight feeling of paranoia overtook me as I realized a text message from someone in the past could just pop up on my phone. I grabbed the dogs, jumped into my Chevy Tahoe, and sped off to the airport. After not being behind the wheel of a vehicle for over a month, I was driving around one of the largest international airports in the country, trying to find a black Lincoln Town Car. I went to the intersection the driver had mentioned, saw a parking lot and pulled in. It was a sea of black Town Cars. After about an hour - I actually found the guy - gave him $50 and made my way back home. So much for Day One.

I'm not sure how Sierra Tucson could possibly prepare anyone for "reentry." I likened the experience to being handed a parachute as you're being thrown out of an airplane and trying to put the parachute on while free-falling. Yes, I had the tools now. What I didn't have was the structure of my days. I wasn't surrounded by friends who could relate to everything I was feeling. I couldn't walk to my daily therapy appointments. And there would be no pudding at dinner! I had to make my own decisions again. The fact that my dog didn't trust me was nothing compared to the fact that I didn't necessarily trust myself.

I planned my return on a Thursday, allowing myself a long weekend for readjustment to civilian life. That was not to be! I hit the ground running, scheduling several business meetings the next day. I planned to meet with my staff in the morning, as well, to get them started on a new project. I also had to meet with my bookkeeper and check on the financials. I was excited and scared once again.

I worked on mindfulness with a therapist during my stay at Sierra Tucson. He had given me the name of a meditation group in Los Angeles called Dharma Punx. I looked it up upon my return and found out the group included a Buddhist-based recovery program called Refuge Recovery. I had tried 12-Step programs in the past, and, while I wasn't necessarily against them, they hadn't served me well. Turns out the Refuge Recovery meeting was about 15 minutes from my house. I knew that I needed to find another "community," so off I went. I needed the support of others who could relate to what I was going through. The meeting was so inspiring. It was a kinder approach to recovery, and the people were amazing.

Self-care at this point was crucial. I felt the need to create a firewall around me and my sobriety. While I was gone, I instructed my assistant to have my master bedroom painted, the rug and furniture replaced, and a new mattress and box spring installed. I refused to return to the "drug den" I had left behind. I was fortunate that my friends were separate from my partying buddies. I basically had created two lives, so "deleting" one was fairly easy. I cleaned up my phone contacts, blocking anyone who would be a potential trigger. I shut my phone off in the evening so that I wouldn't be triggered by a late-night phone call.

At the same time, I reached out to friends for support. I planned a small gathering with them to introduce the "new me." I stopped at the grocery store to pick up food. As I unloaded my groceries at the checkout, the cashier asked, "Hi! How are you today?"

I looked up at her beaming as I placed the chocolate pudding on the check stand. "I just got out of rehab, and I feel great!"

Elizabeth G.

Recalling the first 48 hours when I left Sierra Tucson is something that I thought would be easy. I thought I would have a lot of clear memories and great insights, yet I seem to keep feeling stumped....

It blows my mind that after 42 days at Sierra Tucson, I still must have been in this post-apocalyptic haze such that my brain has only fragmented memories. Forty-two days may seem like an eternity in treatment, but my brain and body had only taken baby steps, albeit very meaningful baby steps.

My brain and body still had a lot of recovering to do, and that is why my first 48 hours would involve taking myself to more treatment.

Before we get there, I think to appreciate this story I need to give a little context. I came to Sierra Tucson because at 28 years old I was totally broken. My life was a series of mental health and addiction labels strung together. I had severe obsessive-compulsive disorder starting at age 4, eating disorders starting in grade school, and extreme social anxiety to the point I had essentially no lasting social connections through much of my childhood. Suicidality came into the picture around age 11 and became a true obsession of mine that would last until recovery. I have probably researched and concocted enough suicide plans to put me in some twisted version of the "Guinness World Records."

By college, I found booze (pills were an added "bonus") and became unable to stop drinking whatever I tried. Alcohol took over my life, which just fueled the depression and suicidality. Meanwhile, men turned into an addiction of sorts. Shopping turned into an addiction. You could even say chaos itself turned into an addiction.

I had been seeing therapists, social workers, and psychiatrists since I was 15. In college, I was even seeing some of the best clinicians around at a premier psychiatric hospital sometimes four or five times a week. I was almost never without top-quality mental health treatment but was still struggling. Finally, at age 24, I started trying Alcoholics Anonymous after a failed attempt on my life. Yet, I soon discovered that I had so much other baloney going on that I needed to go to treatment because I was not staying sober with AA alone. So, after four more years of trying AA, relapsing, resisting the inevitable, waddling back to AA again, and falling flat on my face dozens more times, I finally got to a state of feeling beyond desperate. Although I was in many ways a high-functioning alcoholic and had a plan to attend graduate school and pursue my lofty academic dreams, I knew I needed to stop drinking for real— whatever it would take. I hit a point where I felt unwilling to jeopardize my career or future just so I could compulsively consume a liquid that was thoroughly destroying me. I was not sure I could beat this thing, but I wanted to fight like hell. So, I begged and pleaded to go to residential treatment and ultimately got the support of my parents.

When I got to Sierra Tucson, I was scared, but I felt safe. I was safe from myself and safe from my toxic environment back home. On the check-in sheets every morning, I wrote notes about how my biggest fear and the thing triggering my thoughts of suicide was returning home and leaving Sierra Tucson. Thus, as it got closer and closer to the day that I had to leave, I was petrified. I did not want to go. I wanted to stay in my room in my nice bed. I loved the Tucson warmth in the spring. I loved the mountains. I loved the constant sunshine. The staff had shown me kindness and love that I really needed. This was my safe place.

Nevertheless, after 42 days, it was time for me to embrace continuing care. Deciding on a continuing care facility can be tricky. One reason I decided to continue treatment after Sierra Tucson is that I knew that I had a lot more work to do. At Sierra Tucson, I saw all the messy behaviors I needed to address, and I needed to give myself space and time so I could have the very best shot at recovery. Also, my therapist and psychiatrist at Sierra Tucson strongly recommended continuing care. I knew that when I brought myself to Sierra Tucson, I was going to take every single suggestion I could because I could not financially afford to come back. Things were bad at home before I left, which made the decision of continuing care treatment a little easier for me. Perhaps I was running away and avoiding a bad situation at home, but in doing so I was also protecting my sobriety and myself, which is what it ultimately did. Sierra Tucson taught me that it was OK to look out for myself and not always feel so gosh darn guilty about it!

After much discussion and painful Family Week meetings with my parents, it was agreed that I was going to a women's trauma and substance abuse treatment center in Orange County, California. The van picked me up early and took me to Phoenix Sky Harbor International Airport. Anticipating the long layover I would have in Phoenix if I flew out of Tucson, I had asked the staff if they would make an exception and let me fly out of Phoenix instead to avoid the temptation of alcohol as I waited for my next flight. I did not trust myself yet.

When I arrived at the Phoenix airport, I felt surprisingly happy and optimistic. On the one hand, I had only expected to be gone from home for 30 days and felt guilty being away so long. On the other hand, at Sierra Tucson, I felt what it was like to heal, and I wanted that momentum to continue. For the first time in my life, I had a flicker of that positive child inside me fighting just to keep going even if it defied all my supposedly "rational" thinking.

I arrived at the women's facility so excited for the prospect of being in California for more healing time. Yet, almost the minute I arrived at my new treatment center, I felt scared and alienated. The other women seemed rough around the edges, and the staff was not nearly as nice or validating. Overall, the general atmosphere felt intimidating. Not to mention, despite being sober already a month and a half, they told me I could not have phone privileges for another 30–90 days depending on my progress, and absolutely no phone privileges until I found a sponsor and had completed my Fourth Step. I nearly lost it. Feeling alienated, alone, and cut off from my comforts, my anxiety surged with a vengeance. The first night I barely slept. I thought I had made a huge mistake.

Fast-forward to today. I'm 21 months sober—yes, me, the girl who could literally never stay sober. Prior to Sierra Tucson, I had earnestly tried five years of meetings, Steps, intensive outpatient programs (IOPs), sponsors from all walks of life—you name it, I tried it. I was a relapse expert. I even remembered people in AA telling me they really truly thought I may be one of the "unfortunates" discussed in "How It Works" in AA's "Big Book," who, short of some miracle or maybe a fantastic development in neuroscience, would stay stuck in a pattern of relapse.

I am here today and I am sober. Not only that, but I went from barely speaking to certain family members and considering cutting off contact with some of them to having a more positive relationship with them. I had all but assumed I would never speak to my mother for the rest of my life after treatment, but now we talk regularly and even laugh together, which we had not done in what seemed like 15-plus years. I think I am someone who needed a lot of time away to get as much separation from both alcohol and my environment as possible.

A lot of my peers in treatment would agree that aftercare is a blessing, even if all it gives you is more time away from your drug of choice and your old environment. For me, aftercare saved my life. It started out terrifying but turned out to be the best thing I ever did. I started with about two months at a trauma recovery center, and then transitioned to their eating disorder center for an additional two months before completing three months of sober living and an IOP.

After leaving sober living and the IOP, they recommended I move across the country for some additional outpatient treatment because of some nuanced issues with my case. It has been some of the most rewarding, helpful work I have done in my 15 years of treatment. It's funny—treatment works a lot better when you are sober, although even when you are sober, it can be hard, agonizing, and essentially like a full-time job in terms of time and energy commitments. It's the pushing through the pain that has given me newfound freedom.

Had you told me when I left for Sierra Tucson that now, two years later, I would still be floating around the country in treatment, I would have laughed in disbelief. Few people, if any, I think have to go to treatment for as long as I have, but I can see clearly that this is the only way I would have had a chance at life. I truly needed every second of every minute of every hour that I spent in aftercare, and I mean that wholeheartedly. That is truly how long it took to sort out my correct diagnoses, get on the right medications, and make a meaningful dent on the trauma that was affecting me so profoundly. Healing can be funny in that regard. It doesn't always stick to a neat and tidy schedule.

My plan now is to finish up the last of my treatment and start graduate school soon. It took me two years of total dedication to my recovery to get here, but it was worth every second. While on this journey, I endured a lot of pain and watched many friends, including my roommate in one of the California treatment centers, die of addiction and related disorders. These painful losses, however, inspire me to use my experience to hopefully help others. While I am in no way a perfect example of recovery and still have times when I struggle, I focus on my dream of becoming a doctor and using my experience to bring positive changes to the way addiction is treated and maybe even find a way to directly help people. Perhaps this sounds trite or idealistic; however, after the total and complete hell I've been through, if I'm alive and sober, it is so truly miraculous that I want others to know that even the most utterly hopeless individuals have hope.

Patty R.

My roommate, or "psycho sister" as we still call each other, and I left Sierra Tucson together after treatment, something I don't think happens often, but our return flights home happened to be leaving at nearly the same time....

We got up at 4 a.m. the day of departure, so it was dark when we met Herb, the van driver, who was going to take us to Tucson International Airport for our 7 a.m. flights. I realized during that drive that having landed at the airport just over a month earlier, when I arrived to go to Sierra Tucson—just before midnight New Year's Eve—and leaving now before dawn, that I would still not know what the area outside of Sierra Tucson looked like in the light of day.

My roommate seemed to be excited to be heading home; I was more anxious. At that time, Sierra Tucson did not serve any caffeinated beverages, so I had been eating healthy and caffeine-free for 30 days, enough time to have it out of my system. I was surprised to see how quickly my resolve for clean eating was tossed aside as I ordered a latte at the airport Starbucks. I also remember thinking that here I was, clean and sober for three and a half years, and the realization as to how quickly I had lost my resolve and changed my mind about a cup of coffee was sobering. The physical effects of that latte were immediate, yet I was grateful for them, as I had a long day ahead.

I had about eight hours of flight time and wait time ahead of me before I would arrive home, and as any addict, alcoholic, or person with a mental illness like me knows, time to think does not always produce positive thoughts. I had not felt supported by my family when I made my decision to go to Sierra Tucson, so I asked a friend to pick me up at the airport when I got back. I remember being worried about how others would react to me since I wanted people to see the change. Yet I was worried that no one would notice. I have since been able to better explain that feeling. In a sense, it was like tuning into a soap opera after not having watched it for some time. I had changed, but the life I was walking back into had not, and, more importantly, neither had my friends nor loved ones.

I had come to an understanding that the person who left home was not the same one who was coming home. I had a deeper understanding about myself, although I was still not sure how I would be accepted or viewed. I had always thought of myself as a square-peg, round-hole, bigger-hammer kind of person, and now I knew it was not about trying to force-fit myself anymore. Instead, it was about finding where I fit in authentically and comfortably, and I had a feeling many of the places in which I was struggling to belong were no longer good fits for me anymore.

I started to put some of the support mechanisms that I had found helpful at Sierra Tucson into place back home. It was not an easy task, as many of the things Sierra Tucson offered were cutting-edge and I lived in a small town in upstate New York. However, I continued searching undaunted and found a yoga class, acupuncture, and even a therapist who offered EMDR (eye movement desensitization and reprocessing). By adding to my already existing support system with these newly found options, I created a new path to recovery that was more holistic and geared to my needs.

Before Sierra Tucson I had no idea what my needs were, and coming home, I was scared that I would not be able to re-create and continue the healing that was started at Sierra Tucson. It wasn't easy, and those first 48 hours were pretty stressful, but I was determined not to waste the hard work and effort I had put into the past 30 days. And now, some 14 years later, I have a life I could have never dreamed possible—all thanks to the groundwork laid 30 days prior to those first 48 hours, and the knowledge that I can do anything if I just take it one day at a time.

Glossary

The Language of Recovery

Addict Mind – A term to describe how individuals who are struggling with substance use disorder are able to rationalize and justify their destructive behaviors and habits.

Adult Children of Alcoholics (ACA or ACoA) – A 12-Step recovery program for individuals who grew up in alcoholic or otherwise dysfunctional homes. The founding principle of ACA is that family dysfunction is a disease that infects individuals as children and affects individuals as adults.

Aftercare – Follow-up care recommended or received after residential treatment. Aftercare can include one-on-one counseling sessions, group therapy, 12-Step programs, or other group or individual support programs.

Al-Anon – A 12-Step recovery program that helps families and friends of alcoholics and drug addicts recover from the effects of a loved one's addiction.

Alcoholics Anonymous (AA) – A 12-Step recovery program founded in 1935 by Bill W. and Dr. Bob in Ohio. AA's stated purpose is to help alcoholics "stay sober and help other alcoholics achieve sobriety."

Annual Alumni Retreat/Sierra Tucson Alumni Retreat (S.T.A.R.) – Sierra Tucson holds an annual retreat for its alumni community every fall. The retreat is a multiday program with speakers, events, support opportunities, and recreational activities designed to reaffirm the connection between alumni and their Sierra Tucson experience, as well as with each other.

Art Therapy – Used in psychotherapy and viewed as a healing and life-enhancing activity that encourages self-expression through painting, drawing, or other artistic endeavors. Art therapy is seen as valuable in reconciling emotional conflicts, fostering self-awareness, and aiding in personal growth.

"Big Book" – The book created by Alcoholics Anonymous founders Bill W. and Dr. Bob, who initially called it Alcoholics Anonymous: *The Story of How More Than One Hundred Men Have Recovered from Alcoholism*. It is from this that AA drew its name. It is informally known as the "Big Book" and outlines the 12-Step program, with which the organization has become synonymous.

Binge Eating Disorder (B.E.D.) – A condition characterized by regular and repeated episodes of binge eating, including consuming unusually large quantities of food in a short time and feeling a loss of control during the binge. Those who suffer from binge eating disorder often experience guilt, shame, and distress following the episode.

Burning Ceremony – A Native American practice in which individuals bring an item to release that represents something from the past in order to be rid of the associated emotions. It can also be a prayer request to release into the universe.

Clubhouse – A generic term used to denote a central location for AA meetings.

Codependency – Indicates a state of being that involves excessive, and often destructive, emotional or psychological reliance.

Co-Dependents Anonymous (CoDA) – A 12-Step recovery program in which people come together around their shared desire for healthy and loving relationships.

Codependents of Sexual Addiction (COSA) – A 12-Step recovery program for individuals whose lives have been affected by compulsive sexual behavior.

Continuing Care – This is the next step after residential treatment and includes recovery services and programs that reinforce the tools established during treatment, thus reducing the chance of relapse.

Daily Reflections – Originally published in 1990, this book is by AA members, for AA members. It is a collection of reflections that moves through the calendar year one day at a time.

Day by Day – Written in 1973, this daily meditation book is for alcoholics and addicts.

Desert Flower – Residents of Sierra Tucson begin their journey in Desert Flower, a secure medical assessment and stabilization unit located in the center of campus.

Dry Drunk – A slang expression that describes a person who, although abstinent from alcohol or drugs, continues to behave in dysfunctional ways.

Eastern Thought – The premise behind Eastern Thought/Eastern Medicine is to treat the whole person, which in mental health includes the interrelation of one's behavioral health with such aspects as family, diet, life stressors, and past experiences.

Emotions Anonymous (EA) – A 12-Step recovery program designed to help individuals work toward recovery from mental and emotional difficulties.

Extended Care – A recommended step-down treatment facility to assist in the transition between residential treatment and life in recovery.

Eye Movement Desensitization and Reprocessing (EMDR) – A form of psychotherapy that emphasizes the role of distressing memories in some mental health disorders and has been shown to be useful in assisting individuals in resolving traumatic experiences. Through bilateral auditory, visual, and tactile stimulation (also known as dual attention stimuli, or DAS), the treatment aims to change an individual's emotional response to a traumatic memory from dysfunctional to healthy by allowing access to adult coping skills and resources.

Family Week – An integral part of Sierra Tucson's Family Program. It is a four-day experience that helps family members clarify their role as healthy, supportive figures and empowers them to set healthy boundaries with each other.

Feelings Form – Distributed daily, this form is completed by Sierra Tucson residents to help assess their emotional state.

First-Step Meeting – When there is a newcomer at a 12-Step meeting, the group will often discuss Step One: "We admitted we were powerless over our [disease] – that our lives had become unmanageable."

Fourth Step – The Fourth Step in 12-Step recovery states, "Made a searching and fearless moral inventory of ourselves." The individual honestly faces his or her past resentments, behaviors, and actions.

Gift of Desperation – Desperation can cut through denial and lead an individual to want recovery more than he or she wants to drink, use, or remain stuck in his or her disease. Those in recovery consider this a gift.

Graduation – When a person successfully completes treatment, he or she is said to have graduated.

Higher Power – A term used by Alcoholics Anonymous and other 12-Step fellowships. Sometimes referred to as a "power greater than ourselves," the term references the idea of a Supreme Being or some conception of God.

High-Functioning Alcoholic – Describes a person who abuses alcohol but appears to function normally despite addiction. Some high-functioning alcoholics drink in secret, and many experience emotional problems that might not be apparent to others.

Incest Survivors or Trauma Survivors Group – A number of groups exist to provide support to victims of incest or trauma, where many begin their recovery through camaraderie and hope.

Intensive Outpatient Program (IOP) – A structured therapeutic setting in which individuals work toward overcoming symptoms of substance use disorder and other mental and behavioral health concerns.

In the Rooms – Members of a 12-Step fellowship often refer to "in the rooms" to describe the support they receive at meetings and in the company of others in recovery.

Life on Life's Terms – Taking life on its own terms means accepting the reality clearly, free from expectations or illusions, and to cease the reliance on substances or habits that serve to help the individual avoid life's circumstances or difficulties.

Lodge Warriors – A name created by residents of Crescent Moon Lodge at Sierra Tucson for the all-male residential accommodation on campus.

Meal Plan – For those struggling with disordered eating, a dietitian creates a daily meal plan that fosters eating recovery.

Meeting – A supportive environment for individuals in all stages of recovery.

Narcotics Anonymous (NA) – A 12-Step recovery program designed to offer support for those with a desire to stop using drugs.

Native American Thought – The American Indian culture believes that all things are related and everything is sacred. This respect for all living things comes from the idea of loving, honoring, and respecting the Creator and Mother Earth.

Obsessive-Compulsive Disorder (OCD) – An anxiety disorder in which people have recurring and unwanted thoughts or ideas that drive them to do something repeatedly.

Pills Anonymous (PA) – A 12-Step recovery program designed to offer support for those struggling with a pill addiction.

Pink Cloud – A phase many people in early recovery experience when they feel a heightened sense of jubilance and excitement associated with their newfound life in recovery.

Post-Traumatic Stress Disorder (PTSD) – A disorder that develops in some people who have experienced a shocking, scary, or dangerous event and may continue to react long after the traumatic event has ended.

Process Group – Consists of people who meet on a regular basis, sharing openly with others to gain a broader perspective on life, as well as acknowledge their own feelings.

The Program – When individuals in recovery refer to the "program," they are referencing the recovery program to which they adhere. Some might follow a 12-Step program, while others might attend support groups and see a therapist regularly.

The Promises – The Ninth Step "promises" are found on pages 83–84 of the "Big Book" of AA and serve as a reminder of the gifts one receives from working a program of recovery.

PTSD Support Group – A place where individuals can discuss day-to-day issues with other trauma survivors. Support groups can also help family members or friends who are caring for someone with PTSD.

Recovery Thought – A thought that is aligned with the recovery way of life – healthy, positive, and solution-oriented.

Relapse – Reverting to old behaviors or substance use patterns during recovery.

Resident – Individuals who are currently at Sierra Tucson for treatment are referred to as residents.

Secondary Treatment – A transitional phase that begins after primary treatment and is supportive but slightly less structured.

Self-Care Cards – Tools that aid in one's recovery and can be used to propel him or her toward positive thoughts and actions.

Serenity Prayer – The Serenity Prayer is the common name for a prayer written by Reinhold Niebuhr, an American theologian. The best-known form is:

God, grant me the serenity to accept the things I cannot change,
Courage to change the things I can,
And wisdom to know the difference.

Sierra Tucson Alumni Support Groups – Peer-led gatherings held throughout the U.S. that are attended by former resident and family member alumni.

Sierra Tucson Alumnus/Alumna – A man or woman who completes residential treatment at Sierra Tucson, or a family member who attends Family Week.

Sierra Tucson "Bubble" – Refers to the safety, security, and absence of judgment felt by many during their stay at Sierra Tucson.

Sierra Tucson Language – An individual becomes familiar with the supportive language used by residents and staff alike on campus during his or her stay at Sierra Tucson.

Sierra Tucson Medallion – A symbolic token distributed to residents at the completion of treatment and family members at the conclusion of Family Week as a reminder of their experience.

Sierra Tucson "Safe" – The feeling of safety and acceptance a resident of Sierra Tucson receives when being his or her authentic self during treatment.

Sobriety Chip – A token picked up at a 12-Step meeting that marks an individual's length of time in recovery.

Somatic Therapist – A therapist who facilitates Somatic Experiencing®, a holistic treatment modality that studies the relationship between the mind and body in regard to one's psychological past. It is used most often for trauma symptoms.

Speaker Meeting – A recovery meeting in which a member of the group shares his or her recovery story.

Spirit Stick – A sacred tradition carried on by Sierra Tucson residents to inspire hope, strength, and support.

Sponsor – In 12-Step fellowships, individuals select other members in recovery to support them in their journey. Sponsors understand the challenges associated with recovery and assist in working the 12 Steps.

Timeline – A life-review tool created by residents of Sierra Tucson to understand the important benchmarks and events that may help explain and make sense of their life's patterns and decisions.

Toolbox – The recovery resources provided to those in treatment that are designed to assist in dealing with life on life's terms.

Trauma Triggers – Experiences that cause someone to recall a traumatic memory.

Triggers – External events or circumstances that might produce fear, anxiety, or panic, leading to discouragement, despair, negativity, or other emotional or psychiatric issues.

Wise Mind – Indicates a balance of the emotional thinking and the rational thinking mind. It balances out logical analysis and emotional distress with intuitive knowing that grasps the bigger picture, rather than just the disjointed parts.

Work the Program – When individuals take to heart and give sincere effort toward weaving the principles, philosophies, and understandings learned through the 12 Steps into their lives, they are "working" a program of recovery.

12-Step Meetings/Program – A community of like-minded individuals in various stages of recovery who gather together to receive encouragement and support, as well as share their experience, strength, and hope.

90 Meetings in 90 Days ("90 in 90") – Since the first 90 days of recovery are critical, 12-Step programs encourage newcomers to attend 90 meetings in 90 days.

If you enjoyed this book

please share your opinion

with others on Amazon.com.

We would love to hear

what you have to say

and greatly appreciate

your support.

SierraTucson.com/NothingChangedButMe
Sierra Tucson Publishing

Made in the USA
Columbia, SC
28 September 2018